What Happens at the RAPTURE?

What Happens When We Die?

MARK G. TOOP

WHAT HAPPENS AT THE RAPTURE?
Copyright © 2015 by Mark Toop

All rights reserved. Neither this publication nor any part of this publication may be reproduced or transmitted in any form or by any means, electronic or mechanical, including photocopying, recording or any information storage and retrieval system, without permission in writing from the author.

The opinions expressed in this book are the author's own and do not necessarily reflect the view of Word Alive Press.

Scriptures marked (KJV) are taken from the Holy Bible, King James Version, which is in the public domain.

ISBN: 978-1-4866-1065-5

Word Alive Press
131 Cordite Road, Winnipeg, MB R3W 1S1
www.wordalivepress.ca

Library and Archives Canada Cataloguing in Publication

Toop, Mark G., author
    What happens at the rapture? : what happens when we die? / Mark G. Toop.

Includes bibliographical references.
Issued in print and electronic formats.
ISBN 978-1-4866-1065-5 (paperback).--ISBN 978-1-4866-1066-2 (pdf).--ISBN 978-1-4866-1067-9 (html).--ISBN 978-1-4866-1068-6 (epub)

       1. End of the world. 2. Rapture (Christian eschatology).
3. Death--Religious aspects--Christianity. I. Title.

BT877.T65 2015   236'.9   C2015-905856-2
                                                                                             C2015-905857-0

Contents

Acknowledgements — v
Preface Scriptures — ix
Introduction — xi

1. Foundational Overview — 1
2. The First Resurrection — 25
3. The Second Resurrection — 27
4. The Event of the Rapture — 35
5. Other 'Mysteries' Exposed — 47
6. Jesus Sets the Captives Free — 61
7. Abraham's Bosom — 67
8. Faith Unto Salvation — 73
9. Points to Consider — 77
10. The Leading of the Holy Spirit — 83
11. The Removal of the Holy Spirit — 89

A Note About the Authorized King James Version — 93
A Note About the Book of Enoch — 97
Appendices: Life and Death Overview — 101
Closing Scriptures — 115

End Notes	119
Bibliography	129
About the Author	131
Search Light Presentation Ministry	133

Acknowledgements

This foundational overview is not based on any specific doctrine stemming from any one or more particular denominations of faith. Nor does it stem from any particular theologians' point of view.

This has been the direct result of a leading by the Holy Spirit, the Spirit that leads us into all truth and righteousness. I acknowledge the working of the Holy Spirit in my life, which has brought forth this work.

Special Thanks

I thank God for my wife Jacquie and my daughter Lindsey, who have been blessings of support and stability in my life and who are a constant reminder of the purpose of this ministry.

Special thanks to Roger Oakland, Larry McLean, and the late Dr. Glen Mclean, whose early video series *The Bible: The Key to Understanding* was a turning point in my life. I have come to know that there are no random 'chance' events—there is a reason for everything.

Special thanks to the late Grace Jacobson, who lovingly gave me my first copy of the Authorized King James Bible—the very same Bible that I have quoted from and have used to formulate this book.

Special thanks to Glen Dow who, by his gracious help in the early 1990s, got me started learning Microsoft Word which has been invaluable to my ongoing research and writing.

Special thanks to Micah Newman, Ryan Bowd, and my wife Jacquie for their proofing and recommendations.

Special thanks to Mike Gendron, founder of "Proclaiming the Gospel Ministries" (Garland, Texas), for his review of the manuscript and for his positive and encouraging comments.

Special thanks to Reverend Tim Acey of Living Faith Pentecostal Church for his review of the manuscript and for his positive and encouraging comments.

Special thanks to Ed Coleman, his wife Betty, and his son Jeffrey for their dedication, devotion, and prayers for this ministry (despite all of the spiritual attacks!).

Special thanks to Colin and Crystal Campbell for their gracious and overwhelming support. The Lord works through various people for His purpose and will to be done—again, there is reason for everything!

I wish to thank all those individuals who have believed in, and have prayed for, this ministry.

Lord bless you all!

Revelation 3:20

Behold, I stand at the door, and knock: if any man hear my voice, and open the door, I will come in to him, and will sup with him, and he with me.

Preface Scriptures

1 Corinthians 2:10

But God hath revealed them unto us by his Spirit: for the Spirit searcheth all things, yea, the deep things of God.

1 Corinthians 2:12-14

Now we have received, not the spirit of the world, but the spirit which is of God; that we might know the things that are freely given to us of God. Which things also we speak, not in the words which man's wisdom teacheth, but which the Holy Ghost teacheth; comparing spiritual things with spiritual. But the natural man receiveth not the things of the Spirit of God: for they are foolishness unto him: neither can he know them, because they are spiritually discerned.

Revelation 3:10

Because thou hast kept the word of my patience, I also will keep thee from the hour of temptation, which shall come upon all the world, to try them that dwell upon the earth.

Introduction

We are told in God's Word that those who are disciples of Christ will receive everlasting life and will never be 'plucked' out of the hand of the Father, or Christ, who are one (John 10:27–30). We are also told that at the end of the Thousand Year Reign of Christ, Satan will be unbound from his chains and will go out to deceive the nations for one last, final time (Revelation 20:7–8). This takes place one thousand years after Armageddon.

If the Rapture takes place before the Thousand Year Reign begins, and the born-again disciples of Christ cannot be 'plucked' out of the hand of the Father, then who are 'they' that are deceived by Satan at the end of the Thousand Year Reign?

We are told in God's Word that an individual must be born again to enter the kingdom of God, and Jesus specifically mentioned that one must be born of the Spirit (John 3:3–7). Not born again in the physical sense. We are also told that the physical, corrupt body (flesh) cannot inherit the kingdom of God (1 Corinthians 15:50).

- Does the physical body lie in the grave to await the Rapture?
- Does the spirit lie in the grave to await the Rapture?

- Does the soul lie in the grave to await the Rapture?
- Is the Rapture the same as the First Resurrection?
- Is there a Second Resurrection?
- Are the Rapture and the Second Coming the same event?
- What happens in the afterlife?

What happens to those who have died throughout history, but never heard of Jesus Christ or the Cross and lived prior to First Coming of Jesus Christ (who was God manifested in the flesh)?

- Is Armageddon the end of the world?
- Will the world be repopulated?
- When does "Judgment Day" happen?
- Does God create a new heaven and earth?

We will explore these questions and more as we embark on a journey of understanding. I invite you to read this brief overview carefully and prayerfully, considering each and every sentence as you contemplate its contents. You may need to read this more than once. All scriptures are quoted from the Authorized King James Bible. I encourage you to use your own copy of this version (or at least a comparative version) to reference all the scriptures indicated throughout this book. Also, I encourage you to read all the information and endnotes at the end of this book, as these contain vital information as well.

I pray that the Lord will bless you and that the Holy Spirit will lead you to all truth and righteousness.

Amen.

Foundational Overview

This overview is intended to demonstrate that there is more to the Word of God than what most people, and what some Christian believers, initially might understand. While many individuals have varying opinions and interpretations regarding death, the Rapture, and the afterlife, the intention here is to look deeper at what the Word of God actually says about this topic.

The first thing we need to recognize is that man was created in the image of God (Genesis 1:27). We also need to understand that man was created in the physical sense consisting of bone and flesh, as well as in the spiritual sense, consisting of soul and spirit (1 Thessalonians 5:23).

Man's physical body was initially created out of the dust of the ground, and then God breathed life (spirit) into the formed body (Genesis 2:7). At this point the first man, Adam, was created. Initially, the first woman, Eve, was formed through the removal of a single rib from Adam while he was put in a deep sleep (Genesis 2:21–23).

It should be noted that both men and women currently have twelve pairs of ribs, the exact same number. However, the removal of a rib in sectional surgical procedures can regenerate in two to three months. God most likely spiritually healed Adam as well. Based on this, men are not "missing" one rib as compared to women. It should be also noted that since the inception point where Adam and Eve were both formed (created), ongoing procreation of humankind has resulted in a current population of about seven billion people on earth (by 2011, according to the United Nations). During the 1970s, the earth's population reached 3.5 billion people. This is exactly half of the current population, and that was only some forty years ago. The one-billion mark was reached in 1804, and it is estimated that the earth's population during the Roman Empire was three hundred million (fifty-five to sixty million within the empire itself)—far from the one-billion mark. So, extrapolating backwards in time, the first man and woman came into being less than ten thousand years ago. Bear in mind that a possible 1.5 billion people perished in the Great Flood of Noah; this has been calculated based on sensible statistics and pre-flood conditions over a period of exactly 1,656 years prior to the flood.[1] Continuing to extrapolate backwards, there had to be a starting point of one man and one woman (in full form).

Based on these simple facts, the theory of *transitional* evolution is simply impossible.[2] In the beginning, God created everything to bring forth "its own kind," which is the procreation of each specific species. This ensures that each specific species remains genetically intact, therefore preventing any possibility of change of one species into another (Genesis 1:11–12, 24–25). This is exactly what we see today.[3]

And so, from the God-given formation of the first man and woman, Adam and Eve brought forth their own kind, humankind, through procreation. And it has continued that way ever since.

Foundational Overview

This brings us to the question of what happens to us when we die. This needs to be answered and clearly understood before we can understand what will happen at the coming Rapture, and also what will happen at the coming First Resurrection and Second Resurrection. As we will discover, these are separate and distinct events; they are absolutely not the same.

In fact, we will discover that the Rapture is a distinct event that precedes the Second Coming of Jesus (for those who don't know what the Rapture is, it is where Jesus Christ returns at a future time to remove only the Spirit-filled believers from the earth).

The First Resurrection will occur at the event of the Second Coming. At this point, the Thousand-Year Reign of Christ will begin. At the end of the Thousand-Year Reign, the Second Resurrection will take place. This precedes the Great White Throne Judgment—also known as Judgment Day.

There are four distinct, historical groups of humanity throughout biblical history. There are different parameters that apply to these specific groups (overview and illustrative chart included at the back of this book). Keep this in mind as we progress through this overview.

As we have covered, God formed man from out of the dust of the ground and breathed the spirit of life into him. When a person dies, the physical body returns to the ground (through the grave) and becomes dust once again.

Genesis 3:19

In the sweat of thy face shalt thou eat bread, till thou return unto the ground; for out of it wast thou taken: for dust thou *art*, and unto dust shalt thou return.

Ecclesiastes 12:7

Then shall the dust return to the earth as it was: and the spirit shall return unto God who gave it.

From these passages of Scripture, it is also plain to see that the spirit of man returns to God immediately after the physical body has returned to the ground to become dust once again. This statement, at face value, seems to suggest that it is equivalently certain that any particular individual is assured of a reunion with God, the Father and Creator, upon death.

However, upon further study of God's Word we come to the full realization that anyone returning to God is contingent on whether he or she has been saved through the provision of the Cross by the Saviour, Jesus Christ, prior to the Rapture, or whether he or she has been subsequently resurrected to life after the Rapture (those left behind). The alternative is that a person could end up in hell upon the spirit and soul being separated from the physical body at death, the soul itself subsequently separated from God forever. This includes all those unbelievers who have died, or will die, throughout all human history prior to the Second Coming. Later in this book we will address this in more detail, and address the matter of those who will take part in the Rapture.

As we have just demonstrated, it is very important to read and understand Scripture within the context of other Scriptures of God's Word. Serious misunderstandings and doctrinal error can occur by erroneously proclaiming a premise as absolute fact on the basis of one Scripture alone. Having said that, we have just learned that the body returns to the earth and the spirit *itself* returns back to God upon death—but what about the soul? What actually happens at death?

THE METAPHYSICAL SIDE OF MAN

At this point we are going to take a closer look at the two main spiritual components of a human being: the *spirit* and the *soul*. The third component, already covered, is the physical body—flesh and bone.

It is vitally important to understand that the spirit and the soul are two separate, metaphysical components, yet both spiritually connected. The spirit is the metaphysical component that can connect an individual to God. As we saw earlier, God breathed life into the physical body formed from the dust of the ground. The word spirit found in the Old Testament is derived from the Hebrew word *ruwach* which means *wind*, *breath*, and *exhalation*. Despite the fact that we lost full fellowship with God through the fall of Adam and Eve at the Garden of Eden in our distant past, we can still have a spiritual connection by way of our spirit and the Holy Spirit today. It is through this connection that an intimate relationship can be established with our Lord and Saviour, Jesus Christ.

John 4:23–24

> But the hour cometh, and now is, when the true worshippers shall worship the Father in spirit and in truth: for the Father seeketh such to worship him. God *is* a Spirit: and they that worship him must worship *him* in spirit and in truth.

On the other hand, the metaphysical component of the soul connects to the physical body of an individual. Separation of the soul from the physical body occurs at the point of the finality of death (Genesis 35:18). The soul represents the essence of the whole person. The soul is the centre of three other subcomponents consisting of mind (including intellect and personality), will, and emotions (Job 38:25; Psalm 43:5; Jeremiah 13:17).

In a fallen world, the soul is corrupted by sin. This is the natural state of man. For a soul to be saved, one must first be born again. This is not a rebirth in the physical realm; this is a rebirth in the spiritual realm.

John 3:5-8

> Jesus answered, Verily, verily, I say unto thee, Except a man be born of water and *of* the Spirit, he cannot enter into the kingdom of God. That which is born of the flesh is flesh; and that which is born of the Spirit is spirit. Marvel not that I said unto thee, Ye must be born again. The wind bloweth where it listeth, and thou hearest the sound thereof, but canst not tell whence it cometh, and whither it goeth: so is every one that is born of the Spirit.

Here, Jesus makes it absolutely clear that a person must be born of water (a physical, natural birth) as well as born of the Spirit (a rebirth of the spirit). This rebirth of the spirit (of man) is accomplished through the Spirit (capital S)—the Spirit of God, the Holy Spirit. An obvious example of this is that Jesus was a result of Immaculate Conception via the Holy Spirit and a virgin woman, Mary. The unique aspect of this particular event was that physical sex did not actually occur, and therefore Jesus was born uncontaminated (without sin), separate from the contaminated, historical bloodline of Adam.[4]

This rebirth of man's spirit, being born again, is absolutely necessary before one can enter into the Kingdom of Heaven upon death. Notice Jesus does not state that the soul is reborn. He clearly states that the spirit must be reborn.

An individual can be saved through the provision of the Cross, but there is also a working out of one's salvation along the path of one's spiritual walk. This is not to be confused with the fact that we are saved through the grace of God and not through the works of man (Ephesians 2:8–9). By faith, salvation is a free gift to humanity. However, at the point of one's salvation, one must pick up the cross and follow Jesus. Along the path of the spiritual walk, one begins as a "baby" Christian, then progresses to an "adolescent" Christian, continuing to mature and conform to the perfect will of God. Finally, one enters into discipleship. Yes, we become (or should become) disciples in Christ—just like the original disciples did, with the obvious exception of Judas Iscariot.[5]

Philippians 2:12

> Wherefore, my beloved, as ye have always obeyed, not as in my presence only, but now much more in my absence, work out your own salvation with fear and trembling.

Now, the maturation process I stated above is not guaranteed. There is a big *if* to this desired outcome. Not all Christians, or self-professed Christians, proceed in this direction.

After the spirit of man is reborn, the soul continues to struggle with sin. This is because the soul is very much connected to the body. The body (the flesh) is also corrupted due to our fallen nature. Despite this ongoing—and at times overwhelming—influence, the soul can be brought in line with the regenerated (born-again) spirit. This is achieved through faith, forgiveness, repentance, and the continued renewing of the mind both through prayer (the communication line of man's spirit connecting through the Holy Spirit) and the reading and studying of the Word of God (revelations of spiritual knowledge realized through the Holy Spirit). Read Romans 12:2; Titus 3:4–7; 1 Thessalonians 5:16–18; 1 Peter 1:22–23.

Matthew 26:41

> Watch and pray, that ye enter not into temptation: the spirit indeed *is* willing, but the flesh *is* weak.

Based on this spiritual revelation, the regenerated spirit is in constant struggle with the fallen nature of the body and of the soul. As stated previously, the soul is comprised of a person's *mind, will,* and *emotions.*

Righteousness and the perfect will of God are not based on emotions. Although God has emotions and created man in his own likeness with the ability to experience emotions, divine righteousness transcends emotions. In a court of law, a judge cannot deliver a final judgment based on feeling. He must deliberate on pure facts. The law must be applied separate from emotion. Likewise, God's universal laws are applied to invoke His perfect will uninfluenced by emotion. Pure, divine righteousness transcends emotion. However, based on His emotions, God the Father wishes that none should perish, but instead desires that all would receive everlasting life through His Son, Jesus Christ.

As believers in Christ, we are to be led by the regenerated spirit, in accordance to God's perfect will via the Holy Spirit. If we are not in step with the Holy Spirit, we are out of step with God's perfect will. We are not to be led by our emotions. Allowing our emotions to control us allows the soul to be in control, and therefore our connection to God through our spirit can be interrupted. Ultimately, we should be led by the Spirit. This includes abiding, walking, and discerning by the Spirit. In a fallen world our emotions cannot be fully trusted.

There is also a deeper facet of our emotions: the heart of man. This is not to be confused with the physical heart of an individual, which delivers and receives the supply of blood throughout the body. There is actually a spiritual heart. The physical heart is the central part of the physical body, while the spiritual heart is the central part of the soul. The heart of man is the origin of our passions and desires, or quite simply our wants and needs. Within the fallen nature of the natural man, the heart is tainted with the presence of sin (Mark 7:21–23).

Jeremiah 17:9

The heart is deceitful above all *things*, and desperately wicked: who can know it?

While man cannot fully understand his own heart, and certainly cannot address, or fully reconcile, the sin that stems from it, God knows the heart of man.

Psalm 44:20–21

If we have forgotten the name of our God, or stretched our hand to a strange god; shall not God search this out? For he knoweth the secrets of the heart.

As explained, with the working out of one's salvation (after being born again of the Spirit), the heart can be renewed to the conformance of God's will. Rather than being influenced by the ways of the world (a fallen world), the passions and desires of the heart can change to seek the ways of God.

Psalm 51:10

Create in me a clean heart, O God, and renew a right spirit within me.

Psalm 119:11

Thy word have I hid in mine heart, that I might not sin against thee.

Mark 12:30

And thou shalt love the Lord thy God with all thy heart, and with all thy soul, and with all thy mind, and with all thy strength: this *is* the first commandment.

Romans 10:10

For with the heart man believeth unto righteousness; and with the mouth confession is made unto salvation.

All of this conforming of the heart is in conjunction with the renewing of the mind through prayer, and the continued searching (and applying) of the Word of God.

As with our emotions, our minds cannot be fully trusted in a fallen world. Our thoughts, intellect, and logic do not necessarily produce absolute truth. This has proven to be true throughout all of human history, time and time again. Our thoughts, intellect, and logic (although God-given and surprisingly wonderful at times) do not produce God's absolute righteousness and His perfect will. If they could, then we could save ourselves from ourselves. We wouldn't need God (the same lie Satan told to Eve in the Garden of Eden, Genesis 3:4–5), and based on this false premise God's perfect plan of Christ's death on the cross as a means for our salvation would become a mockery. Satan attacks through the mind. This is the proverbial front line of the spiritual battleground. It is all about choices. Remember, it was God who gave man freedom of choice. We can either freely choose to accept God, or freely choose to reject God.

Romans 8:5–9

> For they that are after the flesh do mind the things of the flesh; but they that are after the Spirit the things of the Spirit. For to be carnally minded *is* death; but to be spiritually minded *is* life and peace. Because the carnal mind *is* enmity against God: for it is not subject to the law of God, neither indeed can be. So then they that are in the flesh cannot please God. But ye are not in the flesh, but in the Spirit, if so be that the Spirit of God dwell in you. Now if any man have not the Spirit of Christ, he is none of his.

Finally, our will cannot be fully trusted in a fallen world. The ways of the world fully promote individual will, realized through the determination of self. This can be described through many terms such as self-analysis, self-confidence, self-esteem, self-image, self-improvement, self-indulgence, self-proclamation, self-realization, self-righteousness, self-sufficiency, self-worth, and—perhaps the epitome of self—selfishness, self-exaltation, and self-destruction. This is exactly what Satan's goal is for mankind. Satan encourages the ways of the world (versus the ways of God) through the proclamation of self. In a fallen world, our souls (mind, will, and emotions) cannot be fully trusted, and therefore the soul must, on an ongoing basis, be conformed to the will of God.

We are told by God's Word to die to self—not to exalt self.

Matthew 16:24-25

Then said Jesus unto his disciples, If any *man* will come after me, let him deny himself, and take up his cross, and follow me.

For whosoever will save his life shall lose it: and whosoever will lose his life for my sake shall find it.

Galatians 2:20

I am crucified with Christ: nevertheless I live; yet not I, but Christ liveth in me: and the life which I now live in the flesh I live by the faith of the Son of God, who loved me, and gave himself for me.

Our will should conform to God's perfect will. Only good things can result from that. Fear and apprehension to do so stem from the fallen nature rejecting its own change, not to mention Satan's continued persuasive attacks through the mind. Fear is a preventer. It is used as leverage to stop one from acting. The ultimate question is, if God is in control, then what is there to fear? We are reminded:

Philippians 4:13

I can do all things through Christ which strengtheneth me.

Many are familiar with the term "soul searching" pertaining to the idea of being true to one's self. However, as mentioned earlier, one must be led by the Spirit (a regenerated spirit) rather than being led by one's self. We must let go of self and *let God*. In seeking God we come to *know* God. Fear can enter in when we don't know God. If we don't know God, then our trust in God is not established. When full trust is established, our complete assurance in God manifests without fear. We should actually fear God, rather than fear Satan. In this context, the aspect of the word fear changes. Satan instills a *threatening* fear, whereas God commands a fear based on respect.

As a note here, the word soul is derived in the Old Testament from the Hebrew word *nephesh*, which is defined as a soul, living being, life, self, person, desire, passion, lust, appetite, mind, will, and emotion. The word soul is derived 103 times in the New Testament from the Greek word *psuche*. This is the same Greek word from which psychology is derived. Psychology is the study of the *mind, will,* and *emotions* of man (from a secular, scientific and non-spiritual perspective). This is precisely why psychology can only offer band-aid solutions to the human condition, because by our own intellect, we cannot address the root cause of sin, which is simply defined as the transgression of God's laws (His perfect will). It is also interesting to note that many psychologists disagree with each other, using different techniques and applying different theories—all individually proclaiming that they know best. Yet, with the growing numbers of practicing psychologists in recent decades, society seems to be regressing in many ways, rather than improving.[6] This is the direct result of the real presence (and increase) of sin within a fallen world, and our own inability to deal with it (Romans 6:23).

Now, having covered these three main components of a human—body, spirit, and soul—an overall concept needs further defining. There is a significant difference between a believer (born-again) and a non-believer. Believers are spiritually alive (1 Corinthians 2:10–12; Hebrews 4:12). Conversely, non-believers are spiritually dead (Ephesians 2:1–5; Colossians 2:13; Romans 8:6; Matthew 8:22).

For the born-again believer, the inner spirit is now awakened, or is now spiritually aware. For the non-believer, the inner spirit is still present but is unaware, essentially in a state of sleep—actually, spiritually dead, unless it is regenerated, reborn by the grace of God through faith and confession in Jesus Christ as Lord and Saviour.

1 Thessalonians 5:5–6

> Ye are all the children of light, and the children of the day: we are not of the night, nor of darkness. Therefore let us not sleep, as *do* others; but let us watch and be sober.

Pertaining to an actual, physical death, it needs to be clearly understood that death (in itself) is not a discontinuance of existence—it is a separation of existence. For the non-believer, the physical body returns to the earth as dust; the spirit (the life force breathed by God) returns to God from where it originated; and the remaining soul is confined to hell—separated from God until the time of the Great White Throne Judgment (known as Judgment Day). For the born-again believer, the physical body returns to the earth as dust, the spirit returns back to God, and the saved soul enters the body of Christ. As we will discover, the saved soul is then "asleep in Christ" until it is awakened at the Rapture. It is here that a new body is created and united with both the regenerated spirit and the saved soul. This will become much clearer as we continue throughout this book.

A few other points need to be stressed at this time: (1) a doctrine has been taught for some time in various religious circles that is referred to as the "doctrine of soul sleep." I want to make it perfectly clear that this book does not represent this particular doctrine. The defining difference is that the doctrine of soul sleep proclaims that both the physical body and the soul (upon death) are at rest in the grave awaiting a resurrection. As just mentioned, at death, the *body* returns to the earth as dust; the *spirit* returns to God; and the saved *soul* becomes "asleep in Christ" awaiting the Rapture. We will discover that this scenario is actually supported by Scripture. (2) We will also discover that a resurrection *does not* occur at the Rapture. The First and Second Resurrections occur *after* the Rapture; (3) in an alive physical body, both the spirit and the soul do not sleep. While the body may enter into a phase of daily sleep, the spirit and soul remain awake and completely functional (this brings into focus the existence of a conscious and a subconscious). However, both the spirit and the soul depend greatly on the physical health of the body—they can be directly affected, positively or adversely (Psalm 6:2–4). The spirit and the soul can grow weak (Psalm 142:3–6). Obviously so, as death ultimately causes both a physical and a spiritual separation, and (4) while the body is living, the soul and spirit (although connected) can be separated for a time. Both the soul and spirit leave the body upon the finality of death, but the spirit can also leave the body while it is alive. This is known as being "taken up in the spirit" (Ezekiel 11:24; 2 Corinthians 12:2–3; Revelation 4:2) and "out of body" experiences (also referred to as Astral Travel, well known within paranormal and occult circles and practiced in disciplines of Eastern Mysticism). We will look at this in more detail later on.

The following Scriptures confirm three things: (1) the spirit and the soul are two separate, yet spiritually connected, metaphysical components to a human being; (2) the Word of God has power, even to separate the soul and spirit and reveal the intentions of the heart; and (3) three main components to a human are in need of regeneration (spirit), salvation (soul), and recreation (body). All three of these occur by the grace of God, through Jesus Christ via the Holy Spirit.

Hebrews 4:12

For the word of God *is* quick, and powerful, and sharper than any twoedged sword, piercing even to the dividing asunder of soul and spirit, and of the joints and marrow, and *is* a discerner of the thoughts and intents of the heart.

1 Thessalonians 5:23

And the very God of peace sanctify you wholly; and *I pray God* your whole spirit and soul and body be preserved blameless unto the coming of our Lord Jesus Christ.

Titus 3:5-6

Not by works of righteousness which we have done, but according to his mercy he saved us, by the washing of regeneration, and renewing of the Holy Ghost; which he shed on us abundantly through Jesus Christ our Saviour;

TWO DISTINCT GROUPS

Now, consider that some people will die *after* the event of the Rapture during the time of the seven-year Tribulation (the Apocalypse). These deceased individuals will either be in hell, or they will be in the 'grave' (also referred to as a place of death; we will use that form throughout the rest of this book). The ones in hell are obviously the unbelievers, and the ones in the grave (death) are the ones who will reject the Antichrist system and call on the *name* of the Lord for salvation. While some circles of various religious faiths believe the body and/or soul are resting in the grave (the tomb) indefinitely until a resurrection (rising from the literal grave), I want to reaffirm this is not what is presented in this book.

Understand that the Holy Spirit (the restrainer) will also be lifted from earth at the Rapture.[7] Some undecided individuals left behind after the Rapture will decide to proclaim Christ during the Tribulation period by calling on His 'namesake' (by the name of Jesus Christ). These particular individuals will *not* be born again by the Spirit, because the Holy Spirit will be gone at the Rapture (1 Thessalonians 2:6–10). This is echoed in the following Scripture:

John 1:12

> But as many as received him, to them gave he power to become the sons of God, even to them that believe on his name.

There are actually two distinct groups referred to here: (1) those who receive Christ as Lord and Saviour becoming "the sons of God" (the New Testament born-again believers *prior* to the Rapture) and (2) those who "believe on his name" (who come to salvation by his namesake without the Holy Spirit *after* the Rapture). This second group is clearly identified in John 1:12 by the distinct phrase "…, *even* to them…" (separated by a comma—emphasis added). Think of the word "even" as being 'also' in the adverb sense (in addition to). There are actually two distinct 'thems' here. Read this Scripture again, carefully, with this in mind. This is reinforced by the following Scripture:

Romans 8:14

For as many are led by the Spirit of God, they are the sons of God.

Here, it is confirmed that the sons of God (the New Testament born-again believers) are the ones led by the Spirit of God. Since they are "born" of the Spirit, they are the ones who will experience the Rapture.

In John 1:12, "even to them" refers to the remnant (the undecided left behind after the Rapture, right up to the Second Coming). This is clearly described in Joel 2, where (1) the Lord will pour out His Spirit *prior* to all the events described in Joel 2 that will come to pass following the Rapture (the Rapture indicated in Joel 2:16—the joining of the church 'bride' and the 'groom'—Jesus Christ). This is echoed and confirmed in Acts 2:17, where it is specifically cited that the pouring out of the Holy Spirit will occur "in the last days" (prior to the Rapture). (2) Following the Rapture, both wondrous and devastating events will occur due to the removal of the Holy Spirit (this is elaborated in the section "The Removal of the Holy Spirit").

(3) It is following the Rapture that "whosoever shall *call on the name* of the Lord shall be delivered" saved from the second death (the spiritual death). We will confirm this later on, since the first death is a physical death. Those left behind will include the majority of the Jewish population (those other than born-again Messianic Jews)[8] and the remnant (the left-behind Gentiles—those other than Jewish heritage). (4) All of this occurs before the "great and terrible day of the Lord" (referring to the specific event of the Second Coming). Bear these points in mind as we read the following:

Joel 2:28-32

> And it shall come to pass afterward, that I will pour out my spirit upon all flesh; and your sons and your daughters shall prophesy, your old men shall dream dreams, your young men shall see visions: And also upon the servants and upon the handmaids in those days will I pour out my spirit. And I will shew wonders in the heavens and in the earth, blood, and fire, and pillars of smoke. The sun shall be turned into darkness, and the moon into blood, before the great and terrible day of the Lord come. And it shall come to pass, that whosoever shall call on the name of the Lord shall be delivered: for in mount Zion and in Jerusalem shall be deliverance, as the Lord hath said, and in the remnant whom the Lord shall call.

As another important point here:

Romans 10:13

For whosoever shall call upon the name of the Lord shall be saved.

Some might argue Paul is unequivocally stating in this Scripture that salvation requires only to "call upon the name of the Lord." This is not entirely true. This Scripture needs to be put into the context of the rest of Romans 10. The first thing Paul states in verse one is:

Romans 10:1

Brethren, my heart's desire and prayer to God for Israel is, that they might be saved.

Paul is expressing that he is very concerned for the salvation of the Jewish people of Israel. He goes on to say:

Romans 10:9–10

That if thou shalt confess with thy mouth the Lord Jesus, and shalt believe in thine heart that God hath raised him from the dead, thou shalt be saved. For with the heart man believeth unto righteousness; and with the mouth confession is made unto salvation.

We need to recognize that Paul is making this statement at a time that is post-Cross and pre-Rapture. Two things are required to be fully saved by the event of the Rapture: (1) confess with thy mouth that Jesus is Lord and, (2) believe in thine heart that God raised Him from the dead.

Then Paul goes on to say:

Romans 10:11-12

For the scripture saith, Whosoever believeth on him shall not be ashamed. For there is no difference between the Jew and the Greek: for the same Lord over all is rich unto all that call upon him.

Paul is clearly revealing that if anyone *believes* in their heart that God raised Jesus from the dead, they will not be ashamed. Those who will eventually take part in the Rapture will not be ashamed. Paul declares that this is available to anyone, Jewish or Greek (non-Jewish). The Lord does not discriminate regarding ethnic heritage.

Conversely, those left behind at the Rapture (the remnant) *will* be ashamed. They may call on His name after the Rapture, but they certainly did not fully believe in Him before the Rapture. They will come to the horrible realization of their own error when they witness the event of the Rapture has passed them by.

The lesson here is yes, "whosoever shall call upon the name of the Lord shall be saved" (as spoken by the tongue). However, this in itself will not guarantee you a place in the Rapture. You must also believe in your heart.

Again, Paul is very concerned for the people of Israel. He feels that many will "call on His name," but few will actually believe He has risen from the dead. This is very evident in today's world. It is estimated that only three percent of the Jewish population is currently considered to be Messianic Jews (born again). Paul goes on to state in Romans 11 that even the Gentiles (non-Jews) have embraced salvation in Christ, but the Jews (God's chosen and the ones who should know better) remain indifferent and complacent in their unbelief. It is Paul's desire of his heart that the people of Israel come to *full* salvation in Christ.

Also, consider that this second group as cited in John 1:12 is actually divided into two sub-groups: (1) those who come to salvation by His namesake without the Holy Spirit *after* the Rapture (both the 'remnant' and the redeemed Israel) as we have just covered, and (2) those who came to salvation by His namesake during the time of Christ's initial ministry. The temporary 'dwelling' (usually pre-Cross) and the permanent 'indwelling' (mainly post-Cross) of the Holy Spirit are elaborated at the end of this overview, followed by a segment entitled "The Leading of the Holy Spirit." Both of these sub-groups are defined by a distinct three-and-a-half-year period. That is the exact length of the ministry of Jesus, from His baptism in the river Jordon to the time of His crucifixion. And although the Tribulation period itself is a total of seven years (Daniel 9:27), the final half of the seven years is known as the Great Tribulation marked by the blasphemies proclaimed by the Antichrist within God's temple (the "Abomination of Desolation," Daniel 9:27). This midpoint is confirmed in Revelation 13:6, and 13:5 confirms the continuance of the Antichrist as "forty-two months" (the latter three-and-a-half years) when the 'mark of the beast' is implemented (Revelation 13:15–18). The Rapture (and subsequent removal of the Holy Spirit) may occur somewhere between pre-Tribulation and mid-Tribulation (depending on the Lord's specified timeframe).[9] Post-Tribulation is really an unlikely scenario, as many described events need to be fulfilled between the Rapture and the Second Coming (described in point-form later in this book). However, the main point here is the distinct difference between *receiving* the 'permanent indwelling' of the Holy Spirit versus 'calling on the name of Jesus.' As John 1:12 points out, to become a 'son of God' (born-again believer) one must *receive* Jesus Christ. And this applies to different historical timeframes. A basic illustrative diagram (#2) of this is also included at the back of this book. Many of this second, left-behind group will die for rejecting the Antichrist and his system during the Tribulation Period and for proclaiming Christ's namesake:

Revelation 20:4

> And I saw thrones, and they sat upon them, and judgment was given unto them: and *I saw* the souls of them that were beheaded for the witness of Jesus, and for the word of God, and which had not worshipped the beast, neither his image, neither had received *his* mark upon their foreheads, or in their hands; and they lived and reigned with Christ a thousand years.

The First Resurrection

Again, many of these 'Tribulation Saints' will be executed (beheaded) for the "witness of Jesus."[10] They may also experience other forms of death (starvation, disease, war, etc.). Initially, these individuals will be left behind right after the Rapture and they will have a traumatic decision to make: accept the Antichrist (and his system) or reject him and accept Jesus Christ as Lord and Saviour. By this decision they will most likely experience some outcome of death, and then they will remain in the grave until the Second Coming. However, by proclaiming Jesus Christ and by rejecting the Antichrist, they will be rewarded as they are brought back to life and will reign with Christ during the Thousand Year Reign. This is referred to as the First Resurrection:

Revelation 20:5

> But the rest of the dead lived not again until the thousands years were finished. This *is* the first resurrection.

The "rest of the dead" (other than the ones brought back to life) refers to all the unbelievers (including all the *undecided*) who rejected Jesus Christ unto death. This includes all the deceased unbelievers and wicked throughout history prior to the Cross, as well as all those after the Cross who remain in, or will enter, hell right up to the event of the Second Coming. They are *not* in the grave. They will *not* take part in the First Resurrection that starts the Thousand Year Reign; however, they will take part in the Second Resurrection at the end of the Thousand Year Reign just before the Great White Throne Judgment. Quite simply, if it is clearly stated that there will be a 'first' resurrection, then there is a distinct possibility of at least a 'second' resurrection.

The Second Resurrection

To reaffirm, the "rest of the dead" also includes the rest of the deceased unbelievers who will perish *after* the Rapture and end up in hell right up to the event of the Second Coming. This also includes all those (of the left-behind remnant) who will perish during the Thousand Year Reign and who will remain in the grave until the very end. A second world conflict (Revelation 20:8) will occur at the end of the thousand-year period—one thousand years *after* the coming world conflict that will take place at Armageddon (at the end of this current world age). Individuals who succumb to the final deception at the end of the Thousand Year Reign will not end up in hell (it is during this time that hell will be locked up by an angel with a key). Instead, they will also end up in the grave as did the Tribulation Saints between the Rapture and the Second Coming. This particular group will remain in the grave right up until the end of the Thousand Year Reign. At this point, there will be a final separation of this particular group between the saved and the damned at the Great White Throne Judgment:

What Happens at the Rapture?

Revelation 20:6

> Blessed and holy *is* he that hath part in the first resurrection: on such the second death hath no power, but they shall be priests of God and of Christ, and shall reign with him a thousand years.

Those who take part in the First Resurrection, based on their proclamation of Jesus, have obviously experienced the first, physical death, but they will not experience the second death—the eternal, spiritual death. Resurrection means "to be raised up from death." This cannot refer to the event of the Rapture. As we will discover, not everyone will experience the *first death* by the time the Rapture occurs.

The final separation concerning all those who will remain in the grave until the Great White Throne Judgment is confirmed in John 5. Bear in mind that the phrase "for the hour is coming" refers to this final Judgment:

John 5:28-29

> Marvel not at this: for the hour is coming, in which all that are in the graves shall hear his voice, And shall come forth; they that have done good, unto the resurrection of life; and they that have done evil, unto the resurrection of damnation.

Also understand that this is a reference to both the First *and* Second Resurrections. The "resurrection of life" initially happens at the First Resurrection at the Second Coming. Here, when Jesus reclaims the kingdoms of the earth, those who remain in the grave but have proclaimed Jesus as Lord will be "resurrected to life."

Those who remain in the grave but have denied Jesus will continue to remain in the grave for one thousand years, or until the event of the Great White Throne Judgment. Those in hell will also remain there until that time.

The "resurrection of damnation" happens at the Second Resurrection that occurs at the end of the Thousand Year Reign, at the Great White Throne Judgment. Here, all remaining individuals who have remained in either the grave or hell will be resurrected for the final Judgment. The majority of this group will be damned for eternity because it includes all the wicked and unbelievers from all of human history.

There is also a "resurrection to life" that occurs at the Second Resurrection. These are the individuals (of the left-behind 'remnant'—*not* the raptured saints) who may perish during the Thousand Year Reign, but still remained loyal to Christ and His established kingdom on Earth. There is a definite distinction between the raptured saints and the tribulation saints—the latter occurring after the Rapture.

And on this basis, the "hour is coming" (the Great White Throne Judgment) is a completion of the Second Coming of Christ. It is also a final sifting to obtain the ultimate tally of all individuals truly saved (of the left-behind remnant) from Satan's temptation and influence. Remember, Satan is bound for a thousand years at the Second Coming (defeated at Armageddon—Revelation 20:1–2), and then he is *unbound* and loosed to deceive the nations for a final time at the end of the thousand years (Revelation 20:7–10).

Many seem to think that Armageddon is the grand finale to the end of the world. This is not biblically correct, as Armageddon concludes the end of this current world age, and the Thousand Year Reign of Christ ushers in a subsequent world age. Pertaining to the reference to the "end of the world" in Matthew 24:3, 'world' is translated from the Greek word *Aion* which actually means 'an age.'

As a footnote here, at the Second Coming of Christ, those who are *alive* at this time will witness Christ returning to earth with His angels. This occurs following the spiritual victory at Armageddon and subsequent judgment of the nations. This group of humanity is collectively represented as the first Beast of Revelation (kindreds, tongues, nations, armies, and kings of the earth). The second Beast of Revelation represents a specific 'man' known as the "false prophet" (the Antichrist). This man exercises the power and authority of the collective first Beast, given to him by Satan (the "god of this world"). These angels are dispatched to gather out all the wicked individuals to be cast into the 'furnace of fire' (the lake of fire) since hell is now locked with a key. The ones who have called on Christ's namesake and are either resurrected to life or still alive will remain on earth with Him as He sets up His Kingdom on earth to begin the Thousand Year Reign (Matthew 13:41–50).

These individuals proceed to repopulate the earth once again, throughout the thousand years, to a very significant population ("…the number of whom is as the sand of the sea" Revelation 20:8).

Based on these profound facts, the following Scripture makes more sense:

Revelation 20:13-14

> And the sea gave up the dead which were in it; and death and hell delivered up the dead which were in them: and they were judged every man according to their works. And death and hell were cast into the lake of fire. This is the second death.

The Second Resurrection

Just prior to the Great White Throne Judgment, some interesting things happen: (1) the *sea* gives up its dead, (2) *death* gives up its dead (this again is referring to the 'grave' in the ground of the earth, and not of the sea), and (3) *hell* gives up its dead (where the majority of the spiritually wicked/unbelievers are kept). Understand that 'death' and 'hell' are referred to as two separate locations—twice. The third location mentioned here is the 'sea.' Overall, this is absolute confirmation of the Second Resurrection (although not specifically stated as such).

As a note of interest here, the non-canonical Book of Enoch (overview and commentary on page 97) also confirms these three separate locations of the dead:

1 Enoch 22:9-12

At that time therefore, I inquired respecting him, and respecting the general judgment, saying, Why is one separated from another? He answered, Three *separations* have been made between the spirits of the dead, and thus have the spirits of the righteous been separated. Namely *by* a chasm, *by* water, and *by* light above it. And in the same way likewise are sinners separated when they die, and are buried in the earth; judgment not overtaking them in their lifetime. Here their souls are separated. Moreover, abundant is their suffering until the time of the great judgment, the castigation and the torment of those who eternally execrate, whose souls are punished and bound there forever."[11]

The interesting thing about this particular passage is that the three separate locations cited in Revelation 20:13–14 are actually indicated within the first two descriptions in Enoch above. "By a chasm" is actually referring to the first two locations of *death* and *hell*, which we will cover later on, and are in fact separated by a 'chasm.' The third location is described as "by water," an obvious reference to the 'sea.'

However, what is simply amazing is that there is essentially a *fourth* location, "by light," and we will discover that this is really a reference to our Lord, Jesus Christ—the "Light of the world" (John 1:6–11; John 8:12).[12] This fourth location is reserved for the "spirits of righteous" (the Spirit-filled, born-again believers— *fully* separated from the "rest of the dead"). The first three *separations* have been made for the "spirits of the dead." This includes all the unrighteous (who are *spiritually* dead) and also for all the other pre-Cross dead, all separated into the two locations of *death* and *hell*. The passage from Enoch above also mentions the "judgment not overtaking them in their lifetime." The "general judgment" to come in the *future* is the Great White Throne Judgment, which applies to the first three, separate locations (as we saw in Revelation 20:13–14).

1 Enoch 22:12 also confirms that, while all these individuals are referred to as 'spirits,' it is further explained that it is their *souls* that are separated and which are actually, in the end, either saved or condemned for eternity.

It is interesting to note that the Book of Enoch is essentially an Old Testament writing (both a pre-Cross and a pre-Rapture book), especially since this particular book was considered part of official Scripture as early as 3rd century B.C. Taking this into context, the reference to "by light" (the separated souls of the righteous in the body of Christ), and looking from this perspective in history, this is a *future* event of the Rapture to unfold. On this basis, this reference 'by light' is not mentioned in Revelation 20:13–14, because the Rapture has already happened over one thousand years prior to the Great White Throne Judgment.

The Second Resurrection

At this point, after all the dead are given up out of these three remaining separate locations, they are judged by their works. When this is finished, 'death' and 'hell' are cast into the "lake of fire." The 'sea' is simply purged of the dead and remains the 'sea' until the new heaven and new earth are created, excluding the sea (Revelation 21:1). This is the final, eternal judgment. Understand that hell itself is a temporary situation. The 'lake of fire' is an eternal destination—forever.

Revelation 20:15

And whosoever was not found written in the book of life was cast out into the lake of fire.

The book of life contains the names of all those who are to be saved from the eternal lake of fire. Take note that this is not referring to hell anymore. Those names not found are doomed for eternity. These individuals will be resurrected, judged, and damned by another 'set of books,' other than the book of life.

This is the Second Resurrection before the Great White Throne Judgment (at the end of the Thousand Year Reign). All of the dead, from all of human history, will stand before the almighty God. Those who were raptured one thousand years earlier will not be part of this Second Resurrection. The raptured saints have already obtained everlasting life. This is why receiving Jesus Christ is so vitally important now while one is alive.

Revelation 20:11-12

And I saw a great white throne, and him that sat on it, from whose face the earth and the heaven fled away; and there was found no place for them. And I saw the dead, small and great, stand before God; and the books were opened: and another book was opened, which is *the book* of life: and the dead were judged out of those things which were written in the books, according to their works.

The Event of the Rapture

Now, understanding our important foundational premise, let us proceed into a deeper understanding of what happens to those individuals who take part in the Rapture. We have already covered this Scripture in the Book of John:

John 5:28-29

> Marvel not at this: for the hour is coming, in which all that are in the graves shall hear his voice, And shall come forth; they that have done good, unto the resurrection of life; and they that have done evil, unto the resurrection of damnation.

We have established that this is actually a reference to all those who will die and remain in the grave—including all future unbelievers (from after the Second Coming to be resurrected at the Great White Throne Judgment) and all past and future saved individuals (those before the Cross and those after the Rapture—saved by His namesake); those who will die and be in the grave until they are resurrected to life (either at the Second Coming—the First Resurrection, or should they die after the Second

Coming, resurrected by the time of the Great White Throne Judgment—the Second Resurrection). We are also told *not* to 'marvel' at this. Both of these scenarios are not the best-case scenarios to be a participant. These are sobering events. Conversely, the Rapture is a joyous event. These participants will be listed in the book of life, not in the 'other books.'

When we compare the following Scriptures found in 2 Corinthians 5:5–8 with John 5:28–29, a contradiction of terms seems to appear:

2 Corinthians 5:5-8

Now he that hath wrought us for the selfsame thing is God. Who also hath given unto us the earnest of the Spirit. Therefore we are always confident, knowing that, whilst we are at home in the body, we are absent from the Lord: (For we walk by faith, not by sight:) We are confident, I say, and willing rather to be absent from the body, and to be present with the Lord.

So conversely, according to Paul, all those who have *received* Jesus as Lord and Saviour by the Spirit long to be "absent from the body and present with the Lord." They experience this longing while they are still alive. And Paul is really speaking about believers who have received Christ and who have existed after the Cross, or currently exist, prior to the Rapture—because, as we have established, the Holy Spirit is referred to as being present here, but is removed from the earth at the time of the Rapture.

However, also understand that these same born-again believers (upon death) are obviously not going to be in hell, but they are also *not* lying in the grave (place of death) either, and they are not in the sea in the spiritual sense—they are with the Lord, literally in the body of Christ ("present with the Lord"). While their physical bodies may have returned to the earth or the sea, their spirits have returned to God and their souls are with the Lord, Jesus Christ (the reference "by light"). They do not remain in the grave. In fact, Paul goes on to describe what happens to this particular group of deceased born-again believers:

1 Thessalonians 4:13-18

> But I would not have you to be ignorant, brethren, concerning them which are asleep, that ye sorrow not, even as others which have no hope. For if we believe that Jesus died and rose again, even so them also which sleep in Jesus will God bring with him. For this we say unto you by the word of the Lord, that we which are alive *and* remain unto the coming of the Lord shall not prevent them which are asleep. For the Lord himself shall descend from heaven with a shout, with the voice of the archangel, and with the trump of God: and the dead in Christ shall rise first: then we which are alive *and* remain shall be caught up together with them in the clouds, to meet the Lord in the air: and so shall we ever be with the Lord. Wherefore comfort one another with these words.

First, Paul makes an emphatic statement that he does not want the reader to be 'ignorant' concerning them which are 'asleep.' Paul does not want anyone to misunderstand what he is about to say.

Secondly, Paul refers to those who are 'asleep'—those who have died, or have 'passed away.' Paul uses the term 'asleep' to illustrate that, when one dies, this is similar to falling asleep. But more specifically, Paul goes on to say "…them also which sleep in Jesus…" meaning those who have received Jesus as Lord and Saviour and subsequently die, their souls will be 'asleep' in the body of Christ. They are *not* awake—not yet anyway. And as we saw previously, the body (flesh and bone) returns to the earth as dust (via the grave), but the soul is present with the Lord and the spirit returns to God (absent from the grave). And since the soul and spirit both *leave* the body, both cannot be in the grave. Both cannot be in two places at once.

Thirdly, Paul says, "For the Lord himself shall descend from heaven with a shout, with the voice of the archangel, and with the trump of God: and the dead in Christ shall rise first." When the Lord descends from heaven at this point, this is the event of the Rapture. This is not the Second Coming, because at the Second Coming Jesus returns completely to earth. Here, we "…shall be caught up together with them in the clouds, to meet the Lord in the air…" Jesus does not come completely down to earth—we will meet Him in the clouds, in the air.

Fourthly, "the dead in Christ shall rise first" is now confirming that those who were 'asleep in Jesus' are in fact the ones who are 'dead in Christ.' The statement that they "shall rise first" has been completely misunderstood. Many church circles have assumed and taught that this refers to believers 'rising from the grave.' We have clearly established that the soul and spirit cannot be in two places at the same time. The word 'grave' does not even appear in these passages of Scripture. The word 'rise' is not referring to 'going up'—it is referring to 'waking up,' as in 'rising up' in the morning. And to cement this point, Paul clearly states, "For if we believe that Jesus died and rose again, even so them also which sleep in Jesus will God bring with him." When Jesus descends from heaven at the Rapture, Jesus brings the dead in Christ *with* Him. They do not 'rise' from the grave; they *descend* from heaven—while they are still asleep and while they are spiritually in the body of Christ ("which sleep *in* Jesus"). And when Christ descends as far as the clouds in the air, they are then awakened (rise) first.

It needs to be stated that the word 'rise' used here is translated from the Latin word *anistemi* which means to 'stand upright *again*' or 'lift up *again*' (in repetition—exactly what one does each and every morning upon waking up). And *anistemi* also means 'arise'—the opposite of 'asleep.' The derivative prefix *ana* also means 'repetition' and 'reversal.' The root word *histemi* also means 'to stand,' 'appoint,' 'present,' and 'establish.'

Another interesting point is that it is clearly stated: "…them also which sleep in Jesus will God bring with him." Both God and Jesus actively participate in this 'awakening' at the Rapture—not just Jesus alone. Although it is obvious and widely accepted that the Father, the Son, and the Holy Spirit are unified in one perfect accord, it is also widely assumed that Jesus (being at the forefront at the Rapture) initiates this event in the singular sense. This is very important because it is at this awakening, at the integral point of the Rapture, that the regenerated *spirit*, the redeemed *soul*, and the recreated *body* are all united as one saved individual. As we saw previously, this is confirmed (and now even magnified) in 1 Thessalonians 5:23.

Before we continue, it needs to be understood that there is no concept of time when one is asleep. When we fall asleep, the next thing we are conscious of (other than dreaming) is that we wake up. We all then look at a watch or clock to determine the current time.

Paul is illustrating that when one dies, it is the same as falling asleep. And based on this, just as one is asleep, there isn't any concept of time when one is dead. And again, if one is a born-again believer and is 'asleep in Jesus,' when one wakes up there will be no concept of how long they have been dead. No matter if the actual timeframe is one month, one year, decades, or centuries until they are wakened by the trump of God at the Rapture. It will seem like they died (fell asleep) one moment, and awakened the next.

Psalm 146:4

> His breath goeth forth, he returneth to his earth; in that very day his thoughts perish.

The word 'breath' used here is derived from the same Hebrew word *ruwach*, meaning 'spirit.' Once the spirit departs the body (in the finality of death), that initiates the body to begin the process of returning to the earth as dust; the *thoughts* of an individual perish. The person is no longer aware of the realm of the living. Regarding post-Cross, this depends on one of two things: (1) they are subsequently awakened at the Rapture or (2) they become self-aware in hell. We will look more closely at pre-Cross and post-Rapture later on.

Another interesting thing is the fact that those who are 'asleep in Christ' are awakened by the "trump of God"—which is, effectively, a spiritual alarm clock![13]

There is another example of this in Scripture. We are familiar with the event at the Cross where Jesus was crucified and died for all the sins of humanity. Jesus rose from the grave (defeated death) on the third day to return to the right-hand side of the Father in the Kingdom of Heaven (Mark 16:19; Romans 8:34). What is very interesting is that two other individuals were crucified along with Jesus, one on each side of Him. One continued to mock Jesus as the Son of God until his death, but the other defended Jesus and asked Him to remember him upon his death. Jesus replied with a very curious statement:

The Event of the Rapture

Luke 23:43

And Jesus said unto him, Verily I say unto thee, Today shalt thou be with me in paradise.

This is very interesting because Jesus did not actually leave the tomb until *three days* later. On the surface this seems like a contradiction. But it makes perfect sense when you consider that the criminal on the cross, who made a decision to accept Jesus before he died, became a born-again believer—right then and there. And upon his death he fell 'asleep' in the body of Christ—that very 'day.'[14]

2 Peter 3:8

But, beloved, be not ignorant of this one thing, that one day *is* with the Lord as a thousand years, and a thousand years as one day.

Time is irrelevant in God's domain, in His existence. All the converted criminal would have known (and will know) is that he died (fell asleep) and will wake up at the trump of God at the Rapture. Even though at least two millennia will have passed by, to him it will absolutely seem like he will arrive in paradise that very day. So Jesus is in fact true to His Word.

Now this is very important to understand because it is commonly assumed that when one experiences the *finality* of death they are instantly 'alive' and 'conscious' of their heavenly surroundings. I am not disputing that this will happen when one 'wakes up.' But from our own ongoing perspective of time, while the rest of us are living, I am quite confident that God would prevent those (assuming they are in heaven and conscious) from 'looking down' upon us, here on earth. Our friends and family members who have passed on would be absolutely saddened and horrified to see all the sin and evil atrocities happening, day to day, here on planet earth. I am quite sure God would spare His beloved from this ghastly sight. Consider this Scripture:

Revelation 21:4

> And God shall wipe away all tears from their eyes; and there shall be no more death, neither sorrow, nor crying, neither shall there be any more pain: for the former things are passed away.

We will look at some other aspects of this later on. But for now, understand that 'Uncle Tom' or 'Aunt Mary' may in fact be in "a better place" when they passed away (in the body of Christ), but for now, at this point in real time, they are *not* looking down upon us.

Fifthly, as we have established, "the dead in Christ shall rise first," meaning that when Jesus descends from heaven and brings the ones who are 'asleep in Jesus' with Him, they are 'awakened' *first* before another part of the Rapture happens. "…then we which are alive *and* remain shall be caught up together with them in the clouds, to meet the Lord in the air: and so shall we ever be with the Lord." The phrase "…then we which are alive *and* remain…" is referring to all the born-again believers who are alive (not asleep or dead) and 'remain'—who are still 'existing' on earth. This is echoed in 1 Corinthians 15:51: "we shall not all sleep." We are then caught up, or brought up to be together with 'them' (the dead in Christ now awakened) to meet the

Lord in the air. Again, fully understand that Christ does *not* come down to earth at ground level. He descends from heaven as far as the clouds, and we (the born-again believers) who are alive are brought up to the clouds to be joined together with them to be as one complete congregation (the 'bride') in the body of Christ (past and present believers up to this point). Again, this is not the Second Coming. Not everyone will see Jesus in the clouds—only the born-again believers.

Conversely, at the Second Coming, *every* eye will see Him (Matthew 24:30; Revelation 1:7). Those who remain on earth at this time will *not* be overjoyed to see Him.

Many things happen between the event of the Rapture and the event of the Second Coming. Without going into any long and drawn-out detail, here is the condensed breakdown:

- We are all changed in a twinkling of an eye—given new spiritual bodies dressed in fine white linens. This also pertains to those who take part in the First Resurrection at the last trump just before the Second Coming (1 Corinthians 15:52). Note: the 'trump of God' that occurs at the Rapture is not the 'last trump,' the final of the seven *trumpets* during the Great Tribulation.[12] These are separate events.

- We go before the Judgment Seat of Christ to receive our gift and reward of crowns based on the recognized good spiritual works done while we were alive on earth. Anything that has carried with us that is not of God is burned out through the proofing fire. (1 Corinthians 3:11–15; 2 Corinthians 5:9–10; Revelation 3:11–12)

- We attend the Marriage Supper of the Lamb in the Kingdom of Heaven, a celebration of the presentation of the saved 'church bride' before the throne of God. (Revelation 19:7–9)

- At this time, on earth, the Antichrist is revealed. (2 Thessalonians 2:1–4)

- A peace covenant, *confirmed* by the Antichrist, will not remain in effect very long as 'peace' is declared amongst the nations, war breaks out shortly afterward (Daniel 9:27; Jeremiah 6:13–15; 1 Thessalonians 5:3). This coincides with breaking of the first seal (Revelation 6:1–2).

- The Jewish Orthodox Priests will be deceived in accepting the Antichrist as their prophesied Messiah. They currently *do not* recognize Jesus as the Messiah. (John 5:43)

- The Antichrist will perpetuate the deception by performing great false miracles known as *lying* signs and wonders. (2 Thessalonians 2:9; Revelation 13:13)

- The Antichrist orders the Orthodox Priests to stop the sacrifice in the rebuilt temple in Jerusalem and replaces this with idols of worship. This is known as the Abomination of Desolation and occurs midpoint of the seven years. (Daniel 9:27; Matthew 24:15)

- The Antichrist proclaims himself as 'god above all other gods' in the temple. (2 Thessalonians 2:4)

The Event of the Rapture

- The Antichrist institutes the 'mark of the beast' and causes all who reject it to be killed. (Revelation 13:15–18)

- World cataclysms occur with increased intensity (weather, earthquakes, solar flares, and meteors, etc.). Note: there are many references citing future catastrophic events throughout the Bible besides what is cited in the book of Revelation.

- War, starvation, and disease continue towards the climax of world conflict when all the world's armies gather at Armageddon, north of Jerusalem. (Revelation 16:16)

- Jesus returns, leading on a white horse, to judge the nations of the earth—the Second Coming. (Revelation 19:11–21)

- The Raptured born-again believers also return with Him on horses, now fully conscious in their new spiritual bodies and dressed in their new fine white linens (after the Marriage Supper of the Lamb). We become His army. (Revelation 19:14)

- Jesus ends Armageddon and sends forth His angels to gather out all the living wicked on earth. This is the exact opposite of the Rapture, where Christ comes specifically for the beloved redeemed. (Matthew 13:37–51; 1 Thessalonians 1:7–10)

- Jesus sets up the Kingdom on earth to reign for one thousand years. (Revelation 20:4–7)

And lastly, "…and so shall we ever be with the Lord. Wherefore comfort one another with these words" (1 Thessalonians 4:17–18). Despite the fact that the earth is heavily repopulated with the remnant of the ones who take part in the First Resurrection, and Satan is unbound at the end of the Thousand Year Reign to deceive the nations for a final time (to effectively weed out the remnant)—those who take part in the Rapture prior to all of this will be with the Lord forever. This is a special group. We are to take comfort in this.

The end of this age of this world will indeed be traumatic, but those who take part in the Rapture will experience the glory of an eternity with the almighty God who created everything; with Jesus Christ (God in the flesh), the one who died on the Cross for the redemption of our sins; and with the Holy Spirit, the Spirit of life and of all truth and righteousness—the Father, the Son, and the Holy Spirit ("Let *us* make man in *our* image" Genesis 1:26, emphasis added). While life is certainly precious in our world, we cannot imagine all the provisions that await us in the heavenly realm to come.

Other 'Mysteries' Exposed

Now, a few more points need to be mentioned and clarified.

The subject of ghosts and spiritual apparitions is a very complex area of research. It is also fraught with deception and half-truths. There is a clear warning from God that we are not to engage in any such activities that involve Spiritism, Mysticism, and the Occult.

Deuteronomy 18:10-12

> There shall not be found among you *any one* that maketh his son or his daughter to pass through the fire, *or* that useth divination, *or* an observer of times, or an enchanter, or a witch, Or a charmer, or a consulter with familiar spirits, or a wizard, or a necromancer. For all that do these things *are* an abomination unto the LORD: and because of these abominations the LORD thy God doth drive them out from before thee.

The manifestation of ghosts that *seem* to portray the appearance of our dead loved ones is a complete deception of the enemy, Satan, and his fallen kingdom. As we have clearly established, the dead are *currently* in one of three places: the body of Christ (post-Cross), hell, or the 'grave' (pre-Cross). They are not wandering around.

However, what is 'wandering' around are the spirits of the ancient deceased Nephilim. These are referred to as 'terrestrial' spirits in the Book of Enoch, and 'seducing' and 'familiar' spirits in the Scriptures of the Bible. These are the demonic spirits of the kingdom of darkness. They are 'terrestrial' because their place of origin is on earth (not heaven) from the result of the sexual union between fallen angels (ancient 'sons of God' Job 1:6–7; 2:1–2) and earthly women (Genesis 6:2–4).[15] They are 'wandering' because upon release of the Nephilim spirit at death, they have no place to go (Matthew 12:43). The Nephilim were a genetic abomination that had a spirit, but they had no soul (unholy procreated), so they cannot enter the Kingdom of Heaven in the spirit (unholy corrupted and not regenerated). Without the soul, salvation is not possible; and in this absence of the soul, while living, there was also a detachment of emotions (the *mind* and inner *will* also altered). 1 Enoch 7:11–13 clearly describes the Nephilim as having turned to eating humans when food became scarce—and doing so with no emotional thought of remorse (a lack of conscience). Conversely, their spirits do not enter hell until they are spiritually commanded to be sent there. On this basis, unless dealt with, the released spirits of the Nephilim are confined to an existence of wandering the earth. They are also known as 'seducing' because they seek embodiment in other human hosts (demonic possession).

Also understand that the term 'sons of God' is a title given by God Himself. This title has been stripped away from the fallen angels and has been declared over the born-again believers in Christ (as we saw in John 1:12). So the connotation of the term 'sons of God' has radically changed from the Old Testament to the New Testament. The Old Testament reference (citing fallen angels) is also found in Job (1:6–7; 2:1–2; 38:7) and Psalm 89:6.

As a footnote here, Adam is referred to as a 'son of God' in Luke 3:38. However, this must be put into context as the historical lineage of ancient man is extrapolated back to Adam (the first man), as described in this Scripture. Only Adam is referred to as a 'son of God'—not the others. This is because in the beginning Adam was *directly* created by the hand of God. Then Adam fell from direct communion with God at the fall in the Garden of Eden. The others were subsequently procreated through the lineage of Adam. It is basically the same with all of the angels. All angels were *directly* created by the hand of God, and known as 'morning stars.' One-third of these morning stars rebelled against God, led by the chief morning star, Lucifer. It is this group of angels that is identified as the 'sons of God' because they also ended up falling away. So God, in His Word in the Old Testament, differentiates between the disloyal fallen angels (the 'sons of God') and the loyal angels (the *other* 'morning stars'). Of course, all angels were once in full unity as 'morning stars.' And again, the title 'sons of God' is now given to the born-again believers in Christ—a restoration of what God intended through Adam.

Here is a clear reference from the Book of Enoch (which coincides with Genesis chapter 6):

1 Enoch 15:8–9

> Now the giants, who have been born of spirit and of flesh, shall be called upon the earth evil spirits, and on earth shall be their habitation. Evil spirits shall proceed from their flesh, because they were created from above; from the holy Watchers was their beginning and primary foundation. Evil spirits shall they be upon the earth,

and the spirits of the wicked shall they be called. The habitation of the spirits of heaven shall be in heaven; but upon earth shall the inhabitation of the terrestrial spirits, who are born on earth. The spirits of the giants shall be like clouds, which shall oppress, corrupt, fall, content, and bruise upon the earth.[16]

Fallen angels (*former* 'holy Watchers'—also known as 'morning stars,' or simply angels) had originated from the Kingdom of Heaven. Terrestrial spirits had originated on earth. Both are part of Satan's overall deception and fallen kingdom.

These demonic, terrestrial spirits are also 'familiar' because from their point of inception they continue to exist throughout history, knowing every detail of the generations of human existence. So it needs to be clearly understood that *ghosts* are in fact terrestrial spirits who are, by the purpose of deception, impersonating the dead, the deceased loved ones. Just as Satan (and other fallen angels) can transform and take on many different forms (an angel, a human, an animal—a serpent, etc.), terrestrial spirits can transform themselves into the likeness of deceased individuals (humans). The modern term for this ability is called shape-shifting. This creates a seduction of the living, drawing them into the involvement of the practices of the Occult (séances, fortune telling, psychics, witchcraft, etc.). As we saw in Deuteronomy 18:10–12, this is strictly forbidden by God. This is for our own protection.

This is an important point that brings us full circle to what Paul had stated in 1 Thessalonians 4. To be absolutely clear, the reason Paul encourages us not to be concerned about the dead in Christ (or the dead in general), and the reason God absolutely forbids any attempt to contact the dead, is twofold: (1) contact is impossible in the first place because the dead are simply asleep (or in hell in torment) and (2) any *attempt* of contact only opens the door to the spiritual world (in which Satan is a master of deception).

There is also a growing interest in the *afterlife* referred to as near-death experiences. There are many books written on the subject. Many accounts describe people who are 'clinically' dead (as opposed to being 'medically' dead)[17] who apparently have gone into heaven and been greeted by prior deceased family members. Understand that Satan and the fallen angels are also on the 'other side.' In fact, Satan and the Old Testament 'sons of God' have presented themselves, and *still* can present themselves, to this very day before the throne room of God (Job 1:6–7, 2:1–2; Revelation 12:10). So we need to be absolutely careful and discerning as to what we may experience on, or hear about, the 'other side.'

There are real near-death experiences facilitated by God Himself. It is usually angels or Jesus Himself involved—not deceased humans. Conversely, when one thoroughly investigates the variables and parameters of events involving the *afterlife*, the majority of them are not God-initiated.[18] And this, in itself, perpetuates the deceptive seduction into the involvement of Occult activities. We are to test the spirits (1 John 4:1).

As a reminder, upon the finality of death, both the spirit and the soul leave the physical body. However, the spirit has the ability to leave while the body is still alive. While God has taken individuals "up in the spirit," it is not advisable to initiate any 'out of body' or 'astral travel' event by one's own volition (i.e. through Transcendental Meditation, Kundalini, Yoga, etc.). Apart from experiences initiated by God Himself, there is a real possibility of demonic attack and subsequent death. If one engages in these types of activities, one is truly playing with fire. Take note that the discipline of Kundalini (a deeper form of Yoga) is also referred to as the "*Serpent* Power." It was the *serpent* who interfered and manipulated God's intention for Adam and Eve, and proclaimed that they didn't need God—suggesting they could become *gods* themselves (Genesis 3:1–7). Hence, we hear of the *self*-proclaimed terms that describe obtaining a 'higher consciousness' or finding an 'inner illumination.' Satan has many counterfeit religions and philosophies that lead the individual on the path of 'self.'

As an important footnote here, the true prophets of God are always one hundred percent correct. It is God providing the information, or revelation, through them. God is always correct. Conversely, Satan and the fallen angels may have access to information beyond the scope and ability of humans, but even they still don't know everything God knows. Therefore, by this very simple fact, any psychic who is not one hundred percent correct (even off by a fraction of a percent) is not of God. Any psychic who claims a high percentage of accuracy is simply a false prophet operating as an agent of the fallen kingdom (whether they know it or not). And despite the fact that some law enforcement agencies have utilized psychics to help find missing persons, or to solve murders, understand clearly that Satan will do a bit of what is *perceived* to be 'good' in order to achieve his ultimate goal: through deception, to lead people away from a real relationship with God and bring about the eventual destruction of God's created humankind. Satan is not our friend. He is not here to 'help' us.

Another aspect of interest is the epitaph inscription on many old-age tombstones: R.I.P., or Rest in Peace. A form of this phrase in the Hebrew language has been found on gravestones in the ancient Jewish town of *Beit She'arim* dating back to the first century B.C. It was not used in English until the eighth century A.D. and then it became very common within some church traditions during the eighteenth century.

There is also a doctrinal belief that proclaims the soul is separated from the body upon death (the body remaining in the *actual* grave), but that then the soul and the body are reunited at the Great White Throne Judgment. Clearly, the Great White Throne Judgment is an event the born-again, Spirit-filled believer does not wish to attend. This doctrinal belief is, of course, contrary to the clear understanding of the physical body returning to the earth as dust once again. Also, there is a distinct reason we are given *new* bodies when we are "changed in a twinkling of an eye."

1 Corinthians 15:50

Now this I say, brethren, that flesh and blood cannot inherit the kingdom of God; neither doth corruption inherit incorruption.

The sinful and corrupt flesh and body stemming from the bloodline of Adam cannot enter the Kingdom of Heaven.

The intention of the phrase Rest in Peace was initially in reference to the soul finding everlasting rest and peace in the afterlife. However, as the epitaph insignia became more universally used and recognized, there was a shift in this original understanding to a general consensus that it was the body that was to lay peacefully in the actual grave. This happened due in part to the fact that the phrase did not specifically infer the soul, and also because the insignia was easily recognized as a marker for a grave site—and so, the inference to the 'body' instead of the 'soul' resting in peace became widespread.

Yet another aspect of interest is the Scriptural references to the reappearance of certain known, previously deceased, individuals. There is the transfiguration of Jesus on the mountain where, after praying, Peter, John, and James witness Jesus transforming into His full glory, His face shining as the sun (Matthew 17:1–9; Mark 9:2–8; Luke 9:28–36). It is here also where Elijah (Elias in the Greek) and Moses appear in full form while Jesus is in shining glory. Jesus speaks with Elijah and Moses, and then a bright cloud appears and God the Father speaks to the disciples. When the cloud disappears, Elijah and Moses are gone.

What we need to understand here is that God can, does, and will resurrect or 'bring back' certain individuals to earth from time to time. This in no way negates what has already been presented here. God has a specific purpose and plan that He is fully in control of. When one carefully studies this type of event, it always seems to involve great men of God—Elijah and Moses for example. Also, consider Enoch, Isaiah, Ezekiel, Daniel, and John who were raised up (in the spirit) into heaven, shown revelations, and then brought back. Some of these men were also physically taken up. There will be a future time when the two witnesses will be brought back to Earth (in full form) to witness to the world in Israel during the Tribulation. We know from the Scriptures that one witness will be Elijah (Malachi 4:5). Some researchers believe the other will be Moses. I believe the other witness will be Enoch (but that is another point for another overview). These two witnesses will be killed and left for dead in the streets of Jerusalem for three-and-a-half days, when the Lord will raise them up alive again and rapture them back to the Kingdom of Heaven (Revelation 11:3–12). The whole world will witness this event (God knew there would be CNN World News by this time!).

Also, note that three-and-a-half days are not enough time for the body to return to the earth as dust. This also applies to Lazarus, who was dead (asleep) in the grave for four days, but there is a hint that this may have been close to the critical point of a successful resurrection of the *current* physical body (John 11:17).

It should be emphasized that both Elijah and Moses appeared right after Jesus became transfigured, or transformed, in His full glory. In other words, Elijah and Moses were already in the body of Christ prior to appearing on the mountain, and present with the Lord prior to Jesus' birth into the world as God in the flesh on earth. Just as Jesus will bring the 'asleep in Christ' with Him at the Rapture, Jesus also brought the two great men of God with Him, because they were *already* with Him (within His transfigured full glory—the Light of the world).

Jesus also instructed Peter, John, and James to not speak of this to anyone until after sometime in the future when He Himself would be raised from the dead (the ascension from the tomb—the grave).

Take note that both Elijah and Moses are exceptions, in relation to the grave, upon their own natural deaths prior to the Cross—where Jesus defeated death and ascended. God brought Elijah up into whirlwind and he was seen no more (2 Kings 2:1) until the day of the transfiguration—and, until the future day when God will send him back as one of the witnesses to Jerusalem. And God Himself buried Moses in an *unknown* grave in a valley in the land of Moab (Deuteronomy 34:6) and yet he also reappears centuries later at the transfiguration of Jesus on the mount.

As another important footnote here, Jesus Himself had spoken about the dead as being 'asleep.'

John 11:11-14

These things said he: and after that he saith unto them, Our friend Lazarus sleepeth; but I go, that I may awake him out of sleep. Then said his disciples, Lord, if he sleep, he shall do well. Howbeit Jesus spake of his death:

but they thought that he had spoken of taking a rest in sleep. Then said Jesus unto them plainly, Lazarus is dead.

Lazarus was in the 'grave,' actually dead for four days until Jesus 'awakened' him (John 11:17). We must understand that, prior to the event of the Cross, those in the 'grave' (not referring to those in hell) are also asleep.

John 3:13

And no man hath ascended up into heaven, but he that came down from heaven, *even* the Son of man which is in heaven.

Some researchers of the Word would argue (and have you believe) that this statement by Jesus is proof that, to date, no one has 'ascended' into heaven. This is simply not true, as Paul himself referred to 'one' who was taken up into third heaven (the Kingdom of Heaven, 2 Corinthians 12:2). This particular Scripture is also grossly misunderstood.

It is true in the context that no one has ascended into heaven in the 'conscious state' (awake), since all who have died prior to the Cross are either in the 'grave' or in hell. And after the Cross, all who have died are either 'asleep in Christ' or in hell. So technically no one has ascended into heaven—in the absolute conscious sense of the word—after the finality of death. However, God does ascend, from time to time, those who He wants to bring up to third heaven (and bring back) either in the spirit or physically. This includes 'clinically dead' situations. These people are not technically *dead*. This phenomenon is a God-initiated event, not a man-initiated event. And, other than a God-initiated event, no one has ascended into heaven (on their own, or apart from absolute death). No one else is conscious in heaven (not humankind, anyway). No one else is walking around in heaven—no one else is awake until the trump of God at the Rapture.[13]

The disciple John was taken up in the spirit and shown a multi-faceted vision of the future by an angel sent by the Lord. This recorded and retold vision has become what we now know as the Book of Revelation, which is meant to portray the *revealing* of Jesus Christ by the Second Coming (Revelation 1:1–3). In this vision John sees twenty-four *elders* in the throne room of heaven (third heaven).

Revelation 4:4

> And round about the throne were four and twenty seats: and upon the seats I saw four and twenty elders sitting, clothed in white raiment; and they had on their heads crowns of gold.

The term 'elders' never refers to angels. Angels do not sit on 'seats' or *thrones* (although some consider that one type of an order of angels may be referred to as 'thrones'; Colossians 1:16). Angels do not wear *crowns*. The fact that these elders are wearing "white raiment" and "crowns of gold" is a distinct description of *men*, who have received 'fine, white linens' (the garment of salvation—Revelation 3:5; 3:18; 19:8) and 'crowns of victory' (rewards in heaven—2 Timothy 4:8; James 1:12; Revelation 2:10).

These twenty-four elders are in fact representatives of the raptured church (elders are the leadership within church structure under Christ). It is the church that will rule with Christ during the Thousand Year Reign (Revelation 5:10). However, the fact that these elders (men) are seen in heaven by John is clearly signifying that this is a period *after* the event of the Rapture, but *before* the event of the Second Coming. These elders (including the raptured church) arrive in heaven *before* the arrival of the Tribulation saints (compare Revelation 5:11–12 with 7:13–14). This is further amplified by the fact that these twenty-four elders are overwhelmed and overjoyed in their own salvation, and they openly express this bursting gratitude with unrelenting praise (Revelation 5:11–12; 7:10–12; 19:4).

Psalm 115:17-18

> The dead praise not the LORD, neither any that go down into silence. But we will bless the LORD from this time forth and for evermore. Praise the LORD.

This Scripture is a confirmation that the 'spiritually dead' (while living) do not recognize God, displayed through a lack of praise, and the same applies to the 'physically dead' who "go down into silence" (into the deep, dark pit of hell—silenced from the world of the living). Conversely, the Spirit-filled, born-again believers do praise the Lord (while living) and will continue to do so from the point of the spiritual regeneration of their spirits to their eventual awakening at the Rapture, and forever thereafter.

However, it is important to mention here again that those who are in hell are not 'asleep.' This also applies to those cast into the lake of fire, the final destination for the damned. They are not 'in a better place.' Conversely, they are fully conscious. In fact, they are in a state of perpetual torment.

Matthew 13:42

> And shall cast them into a furnace of fire: there shall be wailing and gnashing of teeth.

Other 'Mysteries' Exposed

We are going to revisit this point a bit later when we have a look at Abraham's Bosom.

The bottom line is that God resurrects/takes up who He wants to, when He wants to, for His sole purpose to be fulfilled.

And as a note of interest, Enoch was the first person ever to be raptured (Genesis 5:24; Hebrews 11:5). Enoch did not experience death (the 'first death'). It is stated twice in Genesis 5 that Enoch "walked with God." This is a clear portrayal of a dedicated and loyal disciple of God, and a foreshadow of those who similarly adhere to God's perfect will—who will also participate in the future Rapture that will remove and take up all the true Christian believers. Again, Enoch was another example of a great man of God.

Jesus Sets the Captives Free

We also need to address the fact that Jesus descended into the pit of hell between His crucifixion and the moment He ascended from the tomb to return to the Kingdom of Heaven. Many Scriptures indicate this; we will look at a few.

Matthew 12:40

> For as Jonas was three days and three nights in the whale's belly; so shall the Son of man be three days and three nights in the heart of the belly.

This confirms what was happening to Jesus for those three days following His death on the Cross. Jesus not only took on *all* the sins of mankind (at once) upon Himself—He also descended into the pit of hell (the "heart of the belly"). And yet, He was intact, still sinless, and still divine, able to return to His seat at the right-hand side of the Father in the Kingdom of Heaven.

What Happens at the Rapture?

Acts 2:30-31

Therefore being a prophet, and knowing that God had sworn with an oath to him, that of the fruit of his loins, according to the flesh, he would raise up Christ to sit on his throne; He seeing this before spake of the resurrection of Christ, that his soul was not left in hell, neither his flesh did see corruption.

Some Christians have a hard time witnessing to others, especially in street ministry, prison ministry, or just witnessing to others who have hit rock-bottom in their fallen nature.

I am not suggesting that any one of us is on an equal level to Christ Himself, nor am I encouraging just anyone to enter into the front lines of the spiritual battle (by their own volition). But what I am saying, as a strong point here, is that if God leads you to it—then He will lead you through it. For the born-again believer, it is through Christ, in you, that real victory is achieved. So as long as one is led by the Holy Spirit, it is His purpose and His will that will be accomplished—nothing can stand against you, in the spiritual sense. We need to be prepared that this may involve precarious and intense situations outside our comfort zone. There is a time and place that is ordained by God. Jesus calls us to pick up the cross and follow Him (Mark 8:34).

Now, there was a distinct purpose why Jesus descended into hell:

Revelation 1:18

I am He who liveth, and was dead; and, behold, I am alive for evermore. Amen; and I have the keys of hell and of death.

Jesus descended into hell to seize back the keys to both hell and death (again, two separate locations, the latter being the grave).

As we have established, being truly born again must be through the Spirit. Jesus didn't leave the Holy Spirit amongst those living (and dying) in the world until He returned in the Spirit and *breathed* the Holy Spirit upon the disciples (John 20:22). So essentially, upon His own death on the Cross, Jesus had some unfinished business concerning all those individuals who had died throughout history *prior* to His death on the Cross.

1 Peter 3:18-20

> For Christ also hath once suffered for sins, the just for the unjust, that he might bring us to God, being put to death in the flesh, but quickened by the Spirit: By which also he went and preached unto the spirits in prison; Which sometime were disobedient, when once the longsuffering of God waited in the days of Noah, while the ark was a preparing, wherein few, that is, eight souls were saved by water.

The ones "in prison" are, of course, referring to those in death and in hell. Jesus made a way (a provision) for some of these individuals throughout history to be saved as well.

1 Peter 4:6

> For this cause was the gospel preached also to them that are dead, that they might be judged according to men in the flesh, but live according to God in the spirit.

Not only did Jesus seize back the keys, He preached to the dead! The remaining unsaved in death and hell would remain in prison until such time that they will be revisited.

Isaiah 24:21-22

And it shall come to pass in that day, *that* the LORD shall punish the host of the high ones *that are* on high, and the kings of the earth upon the earth. And they shall be gathered together, *as* prisoners are gathered in the pit, and shall be shut up in the prison, and after many days shall they be visited.

This 'gathering of the wicked in the pit' is the continuous addition of the wicked into hell right up until the time of the Second Coming. Obviously so, as the 'kings of the earth' and the 'host of the high ones' are now punished at this time (the judgment of the nations). They are then "shut up in prison," a clear reference to one of the angels locking the gates of hell (the bottomless pit) closed with a key. Then, they are all 'revisited' by the time of the Second Resurrection at the Great White Throne Judgment ("after many days"—one thousand years). Also, at this point of the defeat at Armageddon (the judgment of the nations), the first Beast and the false prophet (the Antichrist) are cast into the lake of fire (Revelation 19:19–20). This represents the majority of those individuals alive at the time who will remain absolutely defiant to the Lord, even to His unpreventable and glorious second appearance.

So, following His death on the Cross, Jesus descends into hell to visit the dead and the 'captives' that are in 'prison.' He also seizes the keys to both hell and death. The key to hell is given to an angel right after the Second Coming of Jesus and the enemy's defeat at Armageddon.

Jesus Sets the Captives Free

Revelation 20:1-2

And I saw an angel come down from heaven, having the key of the bottomless pit and a great chain in his hand, And he laid hold on the dragon, that old serpent, which is the Devil, and Satan, and bound him a thousand years,

Thus starts the Thousand Year Reign of Christ on earth. Jesus assigns the key to hell to an angel when Satan is bound for a thousand years. Therefore, although somewhat less obvious, the other key—to death (the grave)—is not used until the time of the Great White Throne Judgment, after the thousand years has finished (the Second Resurrection).

Abraham's Bosom

Now we will review the doctrine of belief known as Abraham's Bosom.

The term Abraham's Bosom itself is derived from the term "to lie in the bosom of another," or to lie next to the chest of another. This was especially true in referring to the gathering of a feast where individuals would sit close together on couches around a banquet table (all leaning to the left-arm side, leaving the right free to motion). In the ancient Jewish tradition it was considered a great honour to be the one sitting 'at the bosom' of the master of the house, the one hosting the banquet. This is alluded to in John 13:23.

This ancient tradition was said to have carried into the afterlife, as it was widely thought that the righteous deceased were in attendance of a banquet hosted by Abraham, the father of the nations. Hence, it was widely accepted that the righteous deceased were in Abraham's Bosom. Conversely, the unrighteous deceased were considered to be in hell as we have come to know today. This spiritual train of thought was widely accepted before Christ's death on the Cross.

However, the ancient traditions believed that *Hades* (Greek) or *Sheol* (Hebrew) was where all the deceased would depart to—the unrighteous ending up on one side (the place of torment) in hell, and the righteous on the other side (the place of rest) in Abraham's Bosom. It was believed a great chasm existed between the two sides. As we saw in 1 Enoch 22:10, the reference "by a chasm" refers to these two separate locations (both sides). Some ancient cultures also believed there was a ferryman that would carry certain individuals across this chasm.

Jesus spoke of Abraham's Bosom in the parable of the rich man and Lazarus in Luke 16:19–31. This is not the same Lazarus we saw raised from the dead. Conversely, in this parable, Jesus made it very clear that no one could cross the chasm (Luke 16:26), dispelling the notion of a ferryman. As we have already learned, Jesus went into Hades to take back the keys to *both* hell and death (the two sides)—and to preach to the dead. So Abraham's Bosom (the place of rest) is the side of death, or the grave, where the ones who are 'resting' are also 'asleep' (as we saw in John 11:11–14).

When the rich man, in torment on the side of hell, sees Abraham in the distance with the beggar Lazarus at Abraham's Bosom, he cries out for mercy to Abraham (Luke 16:24). It is Abraham who answers him, not Lazarus (Luke 16:25–26). Even though Jesus Himself states that Abraham is awake and conscious on the side of death, as is the rich man in his torment on the side of hell, He does not indicate that the beggar Lazarus is also awake. But Jesus made it abundantly clear that the other Lazarus in John 11 was in fact asleep in the grave. Again, we need to recognize that different parameters may apply to God's chosen great men of God, as now in the case of Abraham. As another note, just as Jesus went to 'awake' Lazarus (John 11:11)—He obviously went to 'awake' all the dead in order to preach to them.

Some theologians would argue that Jesus shared the parable of Abraham's Bosom to mock the teachings of the Pharisees (the Old Testament Jewish Priests bound by the law, rather than grace), in a sense, using their own Jewish tradition against them. Jesus described the rich man as having worn "purple and fine linen"—a close description of the dress of the Pharisees themselves (Luke 16:19). And it is noted that Jesus tells this parable *after* the Pharisees derided Him, in His presence (Luke 16:14). The word 'derided' meaning 'to mock' or 'to ridicule.' Jesus, indeed, may have been directing the moral of the story right at them. Interesting that the Pharisees (the past church leaders) were so bound by the letter of the law, they could not even recognize their own prophesied Messiah standing before them. This is a clear example of the absolute difference between 'religion' and true 'Spirituality' (operating by the letter of the law alone, and not by the Spirit).

However, despite the fact that Jesus spoke of the Jewish tradition of Abraham's Bosom, two facts remain inescapable before us: (1) Jesus went into Hades to seize back the keys to both hell and death (both sides of Hades), and (2) Hell, death, and the sea (the three locations) will give up the dead within them before the Great White Throne Judgment. The fourth location "by light" is still yet to come at the Rapture.

Some theologians would also argue that accepting the Jewish tradition of Abraham's Bosom is the same as accepting belief in Purgatory. However, this must be kept in perspective by considering that: (1) those in the grave are asleep, so we cannot pray for them; (2) those in the grave are *not* in a state of 'purification' prior to heaven, (3) based on our current point in history, those in the grave got there prior to the Cross; and (4) those who died after the Cross are either 'asleep in Christ' or in hell—they are not in the grave. Again, we cannot pray for them either (any attempt of prayer/contact is in vain and strictly forbidden). It is now clear that ancient cultures, preoccupied with the afterlife and the dead, were simply grossly deceived by Satan's false kingdom (fallen angels and terrestrial spirits) and false belief/worship systems. For example, the ancient Egyptians focused all their living years preparing for the afterlife. Massive pyramids and burial tombs were prepared for the pharaohs. These tombs were filled with all their earthly possessions. Yet, this was all for nothing. It was a lie. Upon death, their possessions remained behind, and their intended destination of paradise unrealized. Their false god Osiris holds the same title as Satan, the Lord of the Dead.

Therefore, the idea of Abraham's Bosom is simply not the same as the idea of Purgatory. What is also very interesting is that Jesus also speaks of a gathering of a banquet in the afterlife—and not only with Abraham, but also with Isaac and Jacob.

Matthew 8:11-12

> And I say unto you, That many shall come from the east and west, and shall sit down with Abraham, and Isaac, and Jacob, in the kingdom of heaven. But the children of the kingdom shall be cast out into outer darkness: there shall be weeping and gnashing of teeth.

This banquet clearly takes place in the Kingdom of Heaven (third heaven). This gathering of the many coming from the "east and west" refers to the Rapture. Obviously so, as all who attend this banquet are now 'awake' and 'conscious' of their heavenly surroundings. So Jesus is actually portraying that the gathering of the Rapture will occur just before this gathering at the banquet. This banquet is actually a reference to the Marriage Supper of the Lamb (Matthew 22:1–14; Revelation 19:5–9). This event takes place in the Kingdom of Heaven, at some point, between the Rapture and the Second Coming of Christ (as we have learned, this is where Christ fully returns to earth to seize back the earthly kingdoms from Satan's control and then begins the Thousand Year Reign).

The reference to 'the children of the kingdom' speaks of those who remain physically alive on earth, also referring to after the Rapture but before the Second Coming (the ones left behind—the remnant). The 'kingdom of heaven' (v. 11) is not the same reference as the 'kingdom' (v. 12). One is heavenly, the other is earthly—obviously so, as it is the "children of the kingdom" who are cast into "outer darkness" (the pit of hell). Both 'kingdoms' are occurring at the same time. And as we have already covered, the Rapture is an event that removes the saved believers from earth, whereas at the Second Coming the wicked are removed by angels and are then directly cast into the lake of fire (or cast into hell, referred to here as "outer darkness," up until the locking of hell) where there will be a conscious torment—"there shall be weeping and gnashing of teeth."

Faith Unto Salvation

The pre-Cross generations of man (while they were alive) received forgiveness for sin through offerings of sacrifice (a selected unblemished, genetically pure animal).[19] They firmly believed in the separation of the righteous from the unrighteous in death—ever looking in faith to the future for the promised coming of the Messiah, the Son of God, who would eventually free them from captivity through His shed blood on the Cross and subsequent ascension from the grave—a promise to come.

However, the selected animal for sacrifice (the blood offering) was only a temporary remedy for sin. This sacrifice would need to be repeated. This offering would cause attention to their sin (acknowledgement and confession of sin) and in an act of obedience petition God for His forgiveness, but this temporary blood offering was not a full atonement for all the sins of mankind. The blood of the animal could not remove or blot out sin. While this act of obedience was indeed a result of one's faith, it was merely a foreshadow of the ultimate sacrifice for humanity.

What Happens at the Rapture?

Hebrews 10:1-5

For the law having a shadow of good things to come, and not the very image of the things, can never with those sacrifices which they offered year by year continually make the comers thereunto perfect. For then would they not have ceased to be offered? because that the worshippers once purged should have had no more conscience of sins. But in those sacrifices there is a remembrance again made of sins every year. For it is not possible that the blood of bulls and of goats should take away sins. Wherefore when he cometh into the world, he saith, Sacrifice and offering thou wouldest not, but a body hast thou prepared me:

And now, the post-Cross generations of man look back to the Cross, in faith, as their full atonement of sin, through the shed blood of Jesus Christ, God in the flesh, in the form of man—the Lamb of God and the final and complete sacrifice (blood offering) to the entire world—a promise fulfilled.

Following the baptism of Jesus in the river Jordan by John the Baptist, the commencement of this global ministry was declared:

John 1:29

The next day John seeth Jesus coming unto him, and saith, Behold the Lamb of God, which taketh away the sin of the world.

The pre-Cross generations had looked forward, to the future, to the anticipated coming of the Lord (and subsequent death on the Cross) and the post-Cross generations look back, into the past, to the fulfilled arrival of the Lord (and subsequent death on the Cross). The finished work of Jesus Christ is the key, central point for all of humanity—the full and permanent atonement of sin, absolute forgiveness and complete salvation from the ultimate judgment and an eternal damnation.

Some would say that the pre-Cross generations had even more faith than today's post-Cross generations, because the coming of our Lord and His subsequent death on the Cross hadn't happened yet. So perhaps today we are without excuse—for it has happened, and yet many have failed to see that, for more than two thousand years, Jesus is still alive and well—and He has not simply faded away. The calendar for the entire world is a daily reminder of His birth as year zero, the commencement of the first year A.D. (B.C.: Before Christ, A.D.: *Anno Domini*—the year of our Lord). Jesus was born a Jewish man in the great nation of Israel. All languages of the earth that read left to right are situated west of Israel. All languages of the earth which read right to left are situated east of Israel. Essentially, all written languages of the earth (with the exception of a few languages based on Chinese characters that read up and down) point to Israel, the birthplace of Jesus.

In fact, Jesus also left us a Comforter—the Holy Spirit, to continue on with us during His earthly absence until the time of the Rapture.

John 14:15-18

> If ye love me, keep my commandments. And I will pray the Father, and he shall give you another Comforter, that he may abide with you for ever; Even the Spirit of truth; whom the world cannot receive, because it seeth him not, neither knoweth him: but ye know him; for he dwelleth with you, and shall be in you.

The pre-Cross generations also experienced the Holy Spirit in their time. However, the 'indwelling,' 'dwelling,' and the more commonly experienced 'coming upon' individual experiences portrayed in the Old Testament were more selective, and usually temporary. And yet, again, the people had great faith.

Today's post-Cross generations, according to the Scriptures above, can receive the indwelling of the Holy Spirit permanently—as Jesus states, "that he may abide with you for ever…and shall be in you" ("in you"—not just dwelling 'with' you).

As a final note of interest, Jesus cites two major events of judgment: the "days of Noah" (Matthew 24:37; Luke 17:22–27) and the "days of Lot" (Luke 17:28–30). He equates the days leading up to both as a mirror image of our future society just before His return at the Second Coming. Both Noah and Lot were spared their own 'great tribulation' (the global flood and the destruction of Sodom and Gomorrah) at the last minute. Both of these events are symbolic of the removal of the true believers just before sudden catastrophic doom. The other interesting thing is that Enoch was cited as being very close to God, and also cited as being the first person in history to be raptured (Genesis 5:22–24). Understand that Enoch experienced extreme tribulations of his time, but he did not experience the 'great tribulation' of his time. So, in essence, Enoch symbolically represents the saved 'raptured saints' (taken before the flood) and Noah the saved 'tribulation saints.' Noah went *through* the deluge, the 'great tribulation' of his time, yet he and his family were saved as well.

We indeed live in a period of grace. And we certainly live in a period of exciting, yet perilous times. Amen.

Points to Consider

Some readers may say this overview has been too complicated. Well, the fact of the matter is that the simple Gospel (salvation in Christ) is exactly that—simple, so simple even a child can understand it. However, also understand that there are deeper and expansive areas of God's Word that also need to be explored and considered. The newly born-again Christian requires 'milk and honey' (like a newborn baby). Conversely, the maturing Christian requires a more substantial diet of 'meat and potatoes'—the 'full meal deal' of the Word.

Hebrews 5:13-14

For every one that useth milk *is* unskillful in the word of righteousness: for he is a babe. But strong meat belongeth to them that are of full age, even those who by reason of use have their senses exercised to discern both good and evil.

The problem lies in the fact that while the Bible is the biggest-selling book in the world, it is also the least-read book—usually sitting on one's shelf at home collecting dust. People tend to take things for granted, and tend to take other people's word at face value without checking and verifying where statements and ideas line up with the Word of God.

There are so many misconceptions regarding the afterlife. In fact, if we were to rely on Hollywood's version, upon death we would all be sprouting wings (turning into angels) and residing in the clouds (this is only portraying first heaven and not the actual Kingdom of Heaven). This is a very limited view of how heaven is really established in three main dimensional realms by the creator God. First heaven is the arc of the sky (contains the clouds); second heaven is the expanse of the universe (all other heavenly bodies of planets, stars, and galaxies); and third heaven is the Kingdom of Heaven, where God's throne is located (read Revelation 21 and 22 for this description). And we need to fully recognize that man and angels are completely separate forms of created beings.

Also, if we were to take all the jokes seriously, it would be St. Peter meeting us at the 'pearly gates' of heaven—not us being met by Jesus Himself.

There are also many other serious errors of doctrine regarding the afterlife within many church circles.

There is the idea of Purgatory, a temporary place of punishment or purification for those who 'die in grace.' As we have seen, this is not supported in the Scriptures of God's Word.

In addition, we the living cannot pray for the dead. As Paul tells us in 1 Thessalonians 4, we do not need to be concerned about the dead. What is done is done. There is no do-over. And as we saw in Deuteronomy 18, we are not to be engaged in any attempt of 'contact' concerning the dead. This is absolutely forbidden. The recent dead (after the Cross) are either asleep in Christ, or they are in hell. Any messages from the 'other side' (apart from God's direct intervention) are a deliberate deception by the enemy.

The Virgin Mary is not our intercessor. Like any one of us, who are sinners and are now born again of the Spirit, at the point of death she is also asleep in Christ. She cannot hear our prayers. She is not omnipresent as God, the Father, is. Mary was human and born into the world of sin—she was also in need of the Saviour. There is a belief that Mary was born through Immaculate Conception like Jesus. This is not supported in Scripture. To the absolute contrary, stemming from Adam, *all* have sinned and have fallen short of the glory of God (Romans 3:23).

1 Timothy 2:5–6

For *there is* one God, and one mediator between God and men, the man Christ Jesus; Who gave himself a ransom for all, to be testified in due time.

There are also some readers of this book who would ask, "What difference does this make? I'm saved and that's all that matters—this information does not affect *me* in any way." Well, that may be true. If you are saved through Christ, then you are saved. But what about those who are not saved? What about those who will be left behind after the Rapture? If a person can honestly say, "I'm saved and that's all the matters," is that person saying others *don't* matter? Is that person saying that going deeper into a relationship with the Lord doesn't matter? And if that is true, then that person has seriously missed the full relationship and calling through our walk with Jesus. We are called, as born-again believers, to proclaim the truth and the gospel to others. We are to go forth and make disciples (Matthew 28:16–20).

This does matter. The information contained in this book may lead someone to the truth. It may be the tipping point to lead someone to salvation. Our own, personal salvation through Christ is important—but it doesn't end there. The 'god of this world' (the false spirit—the deceiver) is influencing secular governments in creating sweeping policies to keep Christianity out of the schools, out of the workplace and out of the public's general sight. If we sit back and proclaim, "I am saved and that's all the matters," then not only are we possibly deceiving ourselves, we may in fact be enabling the system in allowing others to be deceived. This book contains spiritual information meant to be shared with others.

Also, there are those who fear death. I have come to the distinct conclusion that those who fear death do not know where they are going after they die. In this regard, they fear the unknown. For the born-again Christian, there is absolute comfort in knowing where we will be after death. It is here that fear has no place.

Hebrews 2:14-15

> Forasmuch them as the children are partakers of flesh and blood, he also himself likewise took part of the same; that through death he might destroy him that hath the power of death, that is, the devil; And deliver them who through fear of death were all their lifetime subject to bondage.

It is interesting to note that proclaimers of the theory of *transitional* evolution believe that man came in to existence through death. In other words, countless transitional life forms had to die first before man could *miraculously* appear.

According to God's Word, it is the other way around. It was through man that death was brought into existence (Romans 5:12). And more specifically, it was through the direct influence of Satan that man subsequently fell from God's initial intended plan for humanity—and then death came into being. By eating of the Tree of Knowledge of Good and Evil, man fell (against the will of God) into a state of sin (Genesis 2:16–17). What is generally overlooked is that Satan's next step was to have Adam and Eve remain in (locked into) a state of everlasting sin by trying to lure them into eating of the Tree of Life next. God prevented this by removing Adam and Eve from the Garden of Eden altogether (Genesis 3:22–24).

As we see in Hebrews 2:14–15, the power of death through Satan was defeated on the Cross. The death of Jesus Christ is the final and complete sacrifice for all sin.

Romans 6:23

> For the wages of sin is death; but the gift of God is eternal life through Jesus Christ our Lord.

All we need to do is to receive this provision by absolute faith and declare Him Lord and Saviour of our lives.

And for atheists, or the deceived, who claim there is no God, what a horrible realization it will be when they are awakened at the Second Resurrection and called to stand before the Lord at the Great White Throne Judgment. This will be nothing less than utter shock and devastation. Despite all of the intellectual rationalizations of men, no one will be able to escape this appointment—except those who are born of the Spirit.

It is my hope and prayer that this overview has been a source of spiritual revelation for you of the deeper things of God. And as mentioned, I have also included a few overviews regarding the Holy Spirit that follow. The leading, discernment, and gifts of the Holy Spirit are critical to the Christian walk. The Holy Spirit is truly the Comforter that Jesus gave to the disciples and for future generations until the Rapture. Just as God breathed the spirit of life into man, formed out of the dust of the ground, Jesus also breathed the impartation of the Holy Spirit onto the disciples and then declared, "Receive the Holy Spirit" (John 20:22). There are a couple of timeline charts at the end of this book. These charts will help you visualize the historical significance of the four separate groups of humanity and their place in the overall biblical timeline. The presence and subsequent removal of the Holy Spirit is also presented in a visual perspective. These two charts are joined at the hip. I also encourage you to read all the segments contained in the Appendices and End Notes, as these offer important information that will help confirm and expand your overall understanding of this initial overview.

The simple Gospel is what brings us to the knowledge of salvation. How we receive it and what we do with it, however, is entirely a different matter.

The Leading of the Holy Spirit

There was a time when, like some of you, I could not make any sense of the words of the Bible. It seemed so foreign to me. Quite frankly, at times it seemed like complete gibberish.

Since those early days of spiritual naiveté, I have gained a much greater understanding of Scripture. And, although I do not claim to know everything, I have come to the absolute conclusion that the Bible is in fact the inspired Word of God—God-inspired and God-breathed.

These are not the mere words of mere men written by their own mere hands somehow inspired by man's own intellect. If that were true, then man would make the obvious choice and would then follow *man's* 'truths' and would proceed on the journey of the right path that would lead us to the salvation of the world—through *man's* will, through *man's* power, and through *man's* wisdom.

Judging by what we have all experienced throughout history, and by what we now witness daily in the news, this could not be further from the truth. It is through the fallen nature of man (manipulated by Satan) that we, as a collective society, are on the path to destruction.

However, despite the initial fall, God gave us His Word through various men, men of God, throughout our history so that we may have an account of our history—a blueprint for our daily lives and a roadmap for our destiny, and more importantly, a provision of salvation through His son, Jesus Christ.

Just as God breathed life into the formed body of man from out of the dirt of the ground, breathing the Spirit of life into him, God breathed the inspiration of His Word into these men of God so that they would record these timeless words for the rest of us to read, and to understand. This inspiration comes from the Holy Spirit. It does not come from man.

The Holy Spirit breathes life into the Word. The Word comes alive. It is the 'living' Word. And it is by the Holy Spirit that we truly understand His Word. This all comes into focus as we read the following Scriptures from the Book of John:

John 1:1

In the beginning was the Word, and the Word was with God, and the Word was God.

The living Word is with God, and the living Word is God.

John 1:2-3

The same was in the beginning with God. All things were made by him; and without him was not any thing made that was made.

God is the creator of all things. By His living Word He *spoke* all things into existence (Genesis 1). In fact, the word 'universe' is comprised of two words, 'uni' and 'verse,' referring to the 'single spoken sentence.'

John 1:10-11

He was in the world, and the world was made by him, and the world knew him not. He came unto his own, and his own received him not.

God, the creator of all things, came into the world and presented Himself to His created humankind (His "own")—but many did not receive Him. They did not receive Him even despite the fact that He presented Himself in the form of a man and dwelt among us.

John 1:14

And the Word was made flesh, and dwelt among us, (and we beheld his glory, the glory as of the only begotten of the Father,) full of grace and truth.

And that 'form' of a man was Jesus Christ—not only the Son of God, but God in the flesh, the living Word, the Alpha and the Omega, the Lamb (slain from the foundation of the world), the Light, the creator of all things.

Upon our spirit aligning with His Spirit, the key to understanding is presented, unlocking the truths within His Word. We continue to 'see' and 'understand' with a developed, spiritual understanding.

What Happens at the Rapture?

John 16:13

Howbeit when he, the Spirit of truth, is come, he will guide you into all truth: for he shall not speak of himself; but whatsoever he shall hear, *that* shall he speak: and he will shew you things to come.

Who else can show us the "things to come" by His Word, with one hundred percent accuracy?

2 Timothy 3:16-17

All scripture *is* given by inspiration of God, and *is* profitable for doctrine, for reproof, for correction, for instruction in righteousness: That the man of God may be perfect, thoroughly furnished unto all good works.

Who else can perfect us through His inspired Word to conform to righteousness?
Who else can save us from ourselves?

1 Corinthians 1:18

For the preaching of the cross is to them that perish foolishness; but unto us which are saved it is the power of God.

One must receive the Spirit of God to be led by the Spirit. To be walking in the Spirit. To be firmly grounded in stature in the Spirit. One must be born of the Spirit. One must be born again.

John 3:3

Jesus answered and said unto him, Verily, verily, I say unto thee, Except a man be born again, he cannot see the kingdom of God.

John 3:5

Jesus answered, Verily, verily, I say unto thee, Except a man be born of water and *of* the Spirit, he cannot enter into the kingdom of God.

I encourage you to seek the things of the Spirit, and the will of God. I encourage you to confess with your heart and tongue that Jesus Christ is Lord and Saviour of your life. I encourage you to love the Lord with all your heart, with all your mind, and with all your strength. I encourage you to walk in faith and to stand without fear. I encourage you to confess your sins, and to repent of them (turn away from them). I encourage you to pray without ceasing. I encourage you to share the good news of the gospel of salvation to others.

I encourage you to be led by the Spirit.
I encourage you to go forth as a disciple.

The Removal of the Holy Spirit

Pertaining to the aftermath of the Rapture, there are two main viewpoints regarding the presence of the Holy Spirit on earth during the subsequent Tribulation period. Some believe the Holy Spirit will remain on earth, and others believe the Holy Spirit will be removed, along with the raptured, born-again believers, right at the moment of the Rapture. After many years of research, contemplation, and prayer, I personally believe in the latter scenario.

I firmly believe that the 'finger' of the Holy Spirit is the restrainer on the proverbial dam holding back the barrage of evil from completely overrunning our society. As reflected in the news, things are certainly bad out there. And it is obviously becoming increasingly worse each year. However, despite the fact that most people have some idea that the Bible describes even worse events to come in the latter days, most still cannot completely envision the total and utter devastation about to come. When the 'finger' of the Holy Spirit is removed from the dam, the world will be plunged into a state of indescribable fear and horror on a scale never witnessed in history—eclipsing the Great Flood of Noah.

What Happens at the Rapture?

There are many reasons why I believe the Holy Spirit will be removed. Without going into any long and drawn-out detail, I will briefly describe the most important points.

(1) One purpose of the Rapture is to remove the Spirit-filled believers from all or most of the impending twenty-one judgments that will occur during the Tribulation period, the greatest intensity occurring in the final three-and-a-half years of the Great Tribulation period (Revelation 3:10; John 10:27–30). This removal event is entirely based on God's timetable.

(2) The living raptured saints (joined with the awakened saints) will go *up* from first heaven and enter second and third when, at the same time, Satan and the fallen angels are cast *down* from second and third heavens to first heaven exclusively. Although Lucifer and the other fallen angels were initially cast out of the Kingdom of Heaven (due to their rebellion against God's plan for angels to serve the newly created humankind), they have still been able to travel throughout second heaven (the Universe) and present themselves, on occasion, before God in third heaven (Job 1:6–7; Revelation 12:10). We need to understand that their 'place' (*permanent* residence) was forfeited after losing the rebellion (Revelation 12:8), but not their occasional visitations. This will all end at the Rapture. Satan and the fallen angels will be confined exclusively to earth's atmosphere (first heaven), and Satan will be extremely agitated and angry when this happens (Revelation 12:12). He will be like an angry hornet trapped inside a glass jar.

(3) This will be the great 'separation.' Essentially, the righteous will be completely separated from the unrighteous.

(4) The Antichrist, the son of Satan, will be revealed to the world (with all of the fallen angels at his command).

(5) The current increasing UFO phenomenon will be unveiled to the world and the fallen angels will step out of the closet

and will falsely present themselves as advanced extraterrestrials (just as they falsely presented themselves as gods in Noah's time—Genesis 6:1–4; Matthew 24:37). This will be a direct result of the removal and absence of the Holy Spirit. There will be nothing preventing them from stepping out of the shadows where they have remained hidden for so long.

(6) Satan is bent on having man serve angels—not angels serving man. He will do everything in his power to deceive all humanity towards this blasphemous goal. In fact, through his deceptive overtures that 'they' are here to 'help us,' the *intended* end result will be the systematic destruction of God's created humankind. Satan knows he was finished at the Cross. The only thing left he can strive to accomplish is to bring down as many souls with him as possible.

(7) During the seven-year Tribulation period, 144,000 specially selected individuals (12,000 from each of the initial 12 tribes) will be sealed with the 'seal of God' in their foreheads. An angel of the Lord will be sent to administer this seal (Revelation 7:2–4). These individuals will be sealed (insulated) from any personal harm due to the flood of evil brought forth as a result of the removal of the Holy Spirit (the bursting of the dam). I firmly believe that *if* the Holy Spirit were present at this time, then God would *not* find it necessary to protect these witnesses amongst the rest of the world.

Those are my thoughts. Time will tell the whole story as it unfolds right before our very eyes.

In Christ's Service,
Mark G. Toop

A Note About the Authorized King James Version

There are many versions of the Bible available in book stores throughout the world. Newer and revised versions are continually being published. How do we know which versions have retained the purity and integrity of God's Word and which have deviated from it?

All of the scripture quotes and references within all of my writings are quoted from the authorized King James Version (KJV). I do this for several reasons.

First of all, I would like to state that the simple gospel, the message of salvation of Christ, can be found and received in various versions other than the KJV. Some examples are the English Standard Version (ESV), the New International Version (NIV), and the American Standard Version (ASV). Based on this, I am not dogmatically opposed to other versions of the Bible (a so-called King James *only* theology).

Having said that, various versions have deviated from the integrity of the Word. These corrupted versions are found to be absolutely blasphemous. These are versions that twist and change God's Word, where the character of the Almighty God has been altered and maligned, and where the simple gospel, a pathway to a real relationship with the Saviour, Jesus Christ, has been blasphemed and compromised.

As we grow in our relationship with the Lord through our spiritual walk, it is the Holy Spirit that will reveal what is truth and what is not.

Prior to the publishing of the KJV, there was a time when the general population was forbidden to have a Bible, much less able to read one. Imagine, God's people prevented from having and reading His Word. The office of the institutional church was in control, even above the level of power of the ruling kings themselves. The kings were considered in a position of divine rule under God, although subservient to the church leaders who were the proclaimed authority stemming from the *office* of God. The Word was kept behind closed doors and stone walls and used as leverage against both the rulers and the common people. It was the church that became wealthier than royalty by way of the collection of taxes (the institutional church being tax-exempt).

Various men of the Spirit began to challenge this status quo in order to bring the Word to the common people. Men such as John Wycliffe, Martin Luther, William Tyndale, Myles Coverdale, and John Calvin pushed for a refined translation of the original tongues into common English. King James I (soon after his crowning) met with the bishops at the Hampton Court Conference in 1604, summoned forty-seven scholars to work within six separate committees, and encouraged the careful consideration of the ancient texts and former translations to arrive at a mutual consensus of the resulted translation into English. The King James Version was completed in 1611.

I believe this endeavor came about through Divine intervention. I believe this was a major turning point in human history where the Word would eventually be preached unto all nations.

A Note About the Authorized King James Version

This progressive reaching to all four corners of the earth is one of the final signs of prophecy before the Second Coming of Christ.

My first Bible was a copy of the authorized King James Version. It was given to me by close friends who knew I was becoming interested in studying the Word. It wasn't until much later that it was pointed out to me by another friend that serious studiers and scholars of the Word tend to use the KJV as their main reference, whereas many false teachers tend to use any other version but the KJV—and if they do quote from the KJV, it is done quite sparingly.

There are those who claim that the old English is hard to grasp in today's world of slang and simple and at times profane language. I would put to those proclaiming this that the old English is in fact more colourful, more descriptive and reveals far more depth in understanding in its broad scope of communication. We are losing the roots and essence of our own English language as it is gradually being replaced with 'texts' and 'tweets' that offer singular thought statements, and even worse, sterile, cryptic abbreviations. While our TV sets have gone from black and white, to colour, to high definition and even to ultra-high definition, our own language has been going in the opposite direction.

This is precisely one of the reasons some of the new and latest translations are corrupt and void of the Spirit. If it is true that the KJV was a result of Divine intervention, then how is it possible that man, and more specifically any singular man, can improve on it? Despite the fact that the KJV has its own inherent errors of translation,[20] these are merely incidental errors and do not detract from the simple gospel of the salvation message. We have to understand that the original translators (although diligent in their work) were also directly influenced by the mindset of the 16th century. Besides, today, in a modern information age we have the instant ability to access and reference the original Hebrew and

Greek language texts and source of translation ourselves. Recent discoveries of ancient artifacts, manuscripts, and archaeological sites have also contributed more clarity and confirmation to an overall understanding of the Word.

On this basis, overall, I hold to and maintain all quotes and references of Scripture from the authorized King James Version of the Bible.

A Note About the Book of Enoch

Some say the First Book of Enoch is not included in the Bible because it is not the inspired Word of God. However, this text (more specifically the segment of the Book of the Watchers) was widely read between 400 B.C and 300 A.D. and was considered Holy Scripture by some of the early scholars of the Middle East. It wasn't until the Council of Laodicea, starting in 363 A.D., that the text was banned from the official canonization along with a large group of other 'lost books' (some of which may *not* be inspired texts). This banishment was executed by the Church of Rome. But despite this fact, the Ethiopic text has maintained Enoch as part of its official canonization.

Also, the Book of Jude (Jude 14–15) quotes a passage from Enoch (1 Enoch 1:9) nearly word-for-word and precedes this with a paraphrase of 1 Enoch 1:1. Ask yourself, how does *any* passage of Enoch (supposedly an uninspired text) end up included within the official canon of the inspired Word? Why did Jesus quote the Book of Enoch on several occasions? Why did God allow this to happen?

The Book of Enoch was considered to be a lost book until renewed interest in the text surfaced during the time of the Reformation (rebellion of the doctrines of the Church of Rome by the people holding to the actual Word of God) in the 1400s. The official rediscovery was attributed to the famous explorer James Bruce in 1773 returning from Abyssinia with three copies of the Ethiopic text. It had been retained for centuries and read by Beta Israel (Ethiopian Jewish communities who settled in the northern horn of Africa, spoken in the Ge'ez language).

In the early 1900s, portions of the Greek text surfaced, and later, seven fragments of the Aramaic text were discovered in Cave 4 (part of the Dead Sea Scrolls). However, it is portrayed in the text that it was Enoch himself who wrote the text prior to the Great Flood.

Perhaps Satan doesn't want the truths revealed in this text to be known, such as (a) the total genetic manipulation of human and animal kind through a falling away from God's plan and laws; (b) the reality of genetic abominations in our past, such as giants, minotaurs, centaurs, cyclopes, pegasuses, etc.; (c) the truth of the origin of demonic, terrestrial spirits (which has been perpetuated through the ancient customs of Samhain—now known as Halloween); (d) the truth of the origin of astrology, witchcraft, cosmetics, jewelry, and fabrication of metal alloys and weaponry, etc. These are only a few of the *very* serious questions and points for consideration.

On a personal note, I was introduced to the Book of Enoch in the mid-1990s. I was engaged in a serious study of the Word and related research, growing in my faith and a deeper understanding of spiritual matters. After my initial reading of Enoch, I found the text nonsensical. Only several years later, after considering other related research, did the text began to make sense, bringing clarity to controversial areas of study and, surprisingly, actually confirming various elements of the Scriptures of the Bible that many teachers and leaders have simply overlooked—even flat-out dismissed.

Looking back, I now realize my initial lack of understanding of the passages of Enoch was not unlike my initial inability to understand the Bible as an unsaved, secular human being. It is through the Holy Spirit that spiritual matters are brought into focus. So, there was a time when I dismissed the Book of Enoch. Now, its revelations continue to surprise me and have actually strengthened my faith in the Lord and His Word.

Appendices
Life and Death Overview

Human History Prior to the Cross

The Believers:
- Forgiveness of sin though the sacrificial offerings at altars, tabernacles, and temples (temporary by year).
- Upon death, they enter the grave (place of death).

The Unbelievers:
- Continued to live sinful lives, sacrificed unto false gods, and built elaborate temples to worship them (pyramids, obelisks, groves, and circular temples).
- Engaged in human sacrifice (Satan perverted the sacrificial offering).
- Upon death, they enter hell.

Human History after the Cross (until the Rapture)

The Believers:
- Cleansed of sin through the shed blood of Jesus Christ (the final, sacrificial Lamb of the world).

- Upon death, they are asleep in Christ.

The Unbelievers:
- Continued to live sinful lives, followed false religions, involved in secret societies (under Satan's control), involved in witchcraft and Satanism; the undecided (having a form of godly morals, but denied the power of Christ).
- Upon death, they enter hell.

At the Rapture

The Believers:
- The 'dead in Christ' are awakened when Christ descends from heaven as far as the clouds in the air (first heaven).
- The believers, who are alive and remain on earth, are raptured up to meet them in the clouds with Jesus.

The Unbelievers:
- Left behind (including the undecided).

The Marriage Supper of the Lamb (after the Rapture)

The Believers:
- Go before the Judgment Seat of Christ.
- Attend a banquet in heaven in celebration of the saved church 'bride' united with her 'groom,' Jesus Christ (the 'bride' presented to the Father).

Appendices: Life and Death Overview

After the Rapture (before the Second Coming)

The Trib-saints:

- Come to a decision for Christ while still alive (call on His namesake).
- Reject the Antichrist and his system.
- Reject the Mark of the Beast.
- Most will experience death by execution, or other forms of death.
- Upon death will enter the grave (place of death).
- Upon living to the bitter end, will be spared by the return of Jesus Christ.

The Unbelievers:

- Continue to live sinful lives and embrace all false religions and lifestyles.
- Follow the Antichrist and his system.
- Accept the Mark of the Beast.
- Upon death will enter hell.
- Upon living to the bitter end, will be gathered out of the false kingdom by holy angels and cast into the Lake of Fire (hell is locked by an angel).

The Second Coming (Christ sets up His Kingdom on Earth—Satan is Bound)

The Believers:

- The raptured saints return with Christ as His army to defeat the enemy at Armageddon (will continue to be with Christ forever).
- Those in the grave will take part in the First Resurrection.

- Those who are alive will be spared and will reign with Christ for one thousand years.

The Unbelievers:
- Those in hell will remain in hell.
- Satan is bound in chains.
- Hell is locked with a key by an angel.
- Those who remain alive represented by the first Beast (all kindreds, tongues, and nations) along with the "false prophet" (alternate name for the Antichrist) will be cast in the Lake of Fire by angels.

The Supper of the Great God
(after the Second Coming)

The Unbelievers:
- The fowls (birds) of the air feed on the carcasses of millions (the remnant) who will die through war, disease, starvation, and by the sword of Jesus at His Second Coming.

The Thousand Year Reign

The Believers:
- All raptured saints are guaranteed everlasting life with the Lord.
- Those who will survive the Tribulation Period, or who take part in the First Resurrection will be tested one last time when Satan is unbound at the end of the thousand years to deceive the nations for one last time (weeding out the remnant of the previously undecided).

- Upon death (remnant only) will enter the grave.

The Unbelievers:
- Those in hell will remain in hell.
- Those in the grave will remain in the grave (now including the newly fallen remnant—hell is currently locked up by an angel with the key).
- Satan is cast into the Lake of Fire at the end of the thousand years.

The Great White Throne Judgment
(the Second Resurrection)

The Believers:
- If written in the Book of Life, they will have an eternity with the Lord.

The Unbelievers:
- The 'sea' gives up its dead.
- Death (the grave) gives up its dead.
- Hell gives up its dead.
- All those who take part in the Second Resurrection are judged by their earthly works recorded in the 'other books.'
- Death and Hell, with all of the damned, are cast into the Lake of Fire for the rest of eternity.

Special Note:

As we have just covered, there are four distinct groups with different sets of parameters concerning death. We are that special second group that has existed after the Cross and pre-Rapture. We are living in a period of Grace. If you receive Jesus Christ as Lord and Saviour of your life and become born again of the Spirit, and remain alive, you will not experience death upon witnessing the day of the Rapture!

It is an exciting time to be alive, for the day is coming soon!

If, for whatever reason, you are left behind, you will have a second opportunity. But fully understand that you will most likely experience the first death (physical death). This will be a very traumatic period, beyond the imagination of the most horrible scenario one could ever envision.

Nevertheless, if you find yourself left behind and you call on the name of the Lord, Jesus Christ, and stand on that proclamation—rejecting the Antichrist, his system and the mark of the beast, although you may very well die the first death, you will not die the second death (the everlasting spiritual death).

The choice is yours. Peace be with you.

John 10:27–30

> My sheep hear my voice, and I know them, and they follow me: And I give unto them eternal life; and they shall never perish, neither shall any *man* pluck them out of my hand. My Father, which gave *them* me, is greater than all; and no *man* is able to pluck them out of my Father's hand. I and *my* Father are one.

Illustrative Chart Overview

Here is the breakdown on the four separate and distinct groups throughout human history. This is based on the individual's destination at the point of death.

Appendices: Life and Death Overview

First Group
Stemming from Adam, but before the Cross
- Believers: In the grave (death), or in the sea
- Unbelievers: In Hell, or in the sea

Second Group
After the Cross, up until the Rapture
- Believers: Asleep in Christ
- Unbelievers: In Hell, or in the sea

Third Group
After the Rapture, up until the Second Coming
- Believers: In the grave (death), or in the sea
- Unbelievers: In Hell, or in the sea. In the Lake of Fire (point of defeat at Armageddon)

Fourth Group
After the Second Coming, up until the Great White Throne Judgment (Thousand Year reign)
- Believers: In the grave (death), or in the sea
- Unbelievers: In the grave (death), or in the sea

Note: Hell is locked by an angel with the key (Satan bound)
Note: Hell is unlocked at the end of the Thousand Year Reign (Satan unbound)
Death (the grave) is unlocked just before the Great White Throne Judgment

What Happens at the Rapture?

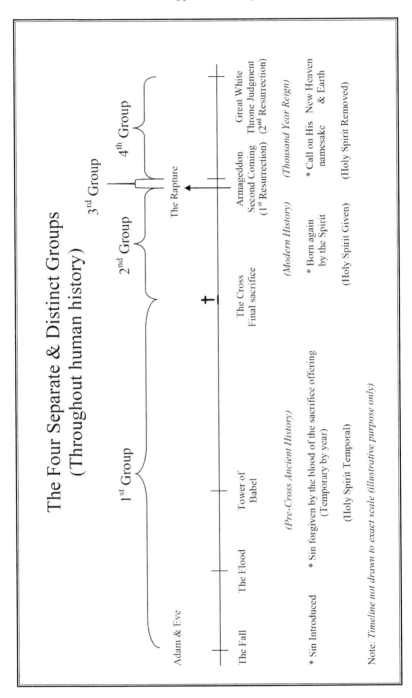

Appendices: Life and Death Overview

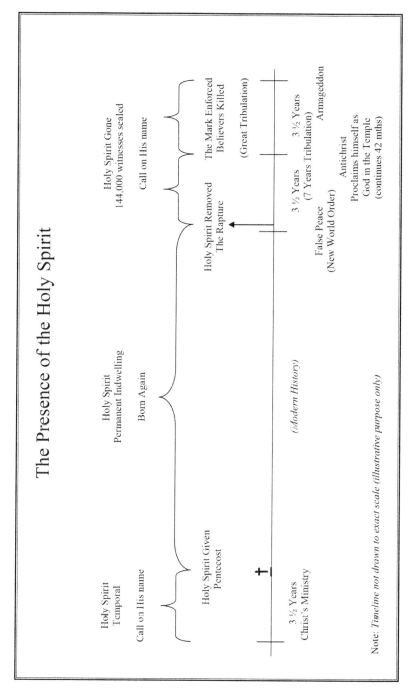

THE RAPTURE / SECOND COMING COMPARISON

This close examination will reveal that these are actually two separate and distinct events. The Rapture has a purpose to present the church to Jesus Himself and to the Father. The Second Coming has a purpose where Jesus executes judgment on the nations and proceeds to set up His kingdom on earth.

- **Rapture:** Jesus is coming *for* His church (John 14:1–3, 1 Thessalonians 4:14–17)
  Second Coming: Jesus is coming *with* His church (Colossians 3:4, Zechariah 14:5, Jude 14, Revelation 19:14)

- **Rapture:** Believers are caught up with him in the air (1 Thessalonians 4:13–18)
  Second Coming: Jesus returns and His feet touch the earth (Zechariah 14:4, Revelation 19:11–14)

- **Rapture:** Christians are taken first, unbelievers are left behind (1 Thessalonians 4:13–18)
  Second Coming: Wicked are taken first, the Tribulation saints are left behind (Matthew 13:28–30)

- **Rapture:** Brings the believers (the bride) to the marriage supper of the Lamb in heaven (Revelation 19:7–9)
  Second Coming: Brings the believers (the bride) to wage war on earth at Armageddon (Revelation 19:11–14)

Appendices: Life and Death Overview

- **Rapture:** Occurs in a twinkling of an eye and too fast for the remaining to see (1 Corinthians 15:52)
  Second Coming: Slow coming, people of the earth see Him coming (Zechariah 12:10, Matthew 24:30, Revelation 1:7)

- **Rapture:** Only Christians see Him (1 John 3:2, 1 Corinthians 15:32)
  Second Coming: Every eye will see Him (Revelation 1:7)

- **Rapture:** No resurrection takes place (1 Thessalonians 4:14)
  Second Coming: Resurrection takes place (Revelation 20:4–6)

- **Rapture:** Can happen at any time (Revelation 3:3, 1 Thessalonians 5:4–6)
  Second Coming: Happens specifically at the end of the Great Tribulation at Armageddon (Daniel 9:24–27, Matthew 24:29–30, 1 Thessalonians 2:3–8)

- **Rapture:** No angels are sent to gather (1 Thessalonians 4:15–17)
  Second Coming: Angels are sent to gather people for the judgment of the nations on earth (Matthew 13:39, 41, 49, 24:31, 25:31; 1 Thessalonians 1:7–10)

- **Rapture:** Jesus descends at the trump of God (1 Thessalonians 4:16)
  Second Coming: Jesus returns after the seventh trumpet by an angel (Revelation 19:11–15)

- **Rapture:** The dead in Christ return with Jesus to receive new bodies (1 Thessalonians 4:14–16)
  Second Coming: Raptured Christians return behind Jesus *with* their new bodies (Revelation 19:11–21)

- **Rapture:** Jesus does not return on a white horse (1 Thessalonians 4:16)
  Second Coming: Jesus returns on a white horse (Revelation 19:11)

- **Rapture:** Jesus returns for the church bride only (1 Thessalonians 4:14–17)
  Second Coming: Jesus returns for the redeemed Israel and the redeemed Gentiles left behind (Romans 11:25–27, Matthew 25:31–46)

- **Rapture:** A message of hope and comfort (1 Thessalonians 4:18, Titus 2:13, 1 John 3:3)
  Second Coming: A message of judgment (Joel 3:12–16, Zephaniah 1:14–16; Malachi 4:5, Revelation 1:7; Revelation 19:11–21)

NOTES:

The Second Coming is referred to as the "The great and terrible day of the Lord" (Joel 2:31). 'Great' because Christ has now come to set up the millennial kingdom, and 'terrible' because of the fiery judgment of the nations and the gathering of the wicked from out of the kingdom into hell by the holy angels. This day is also referred to as "The great and dreadful day of the Lord" (Malachi 4:5). This is also described in Zephaniah 1:14–16 as a day of the Lord's wrath—this is definitely not the Rapture. Revelation

11:15 also describes the seventh trumpet (by an angel) *announcing* the coming seizing of the earthly kingdoms by the Lord—the Second Coming.

There are (3) distinct judgments

1) **The Judgment Seat of Christ**—the judgment of the works of the raptured, born-again saints

2) **The Judgment of the Nations**—implemented at the Second Coming after both the Rapture and the Great Tribulation period, but just before the Thousand Year Reign of Christ on Earth begins

3) **The Great White Throne Judgment**—the final judgment at the end of the Thousand Year Reign that ushers in a new heaven and earth for eternity

Closing Scriptures

1 Corinthians 15:12

Now if Christ be preached that he rose from the dead, how say some among you that there is no resurrection of the dead?

1 Corinthians 15:20-22

But now is Christ risen from the dead, *and* become the firstfruits of them that slept. For since by man *came* death, by man *came* also the resurrection of the dead. For as in Adam all die, even so in Christ shall all be made alive.

1 Corinthians 15:24

Then *cometh* the end, when he shall have delivered up the kingdom to God, even the Father; when he shall have put down all rule and all authority and power. For he must reign, till he hath put all enemies under his feet. The last enemy *that* shall be destroyed *is* death.

What Happens at the Rapture?

1 Corinthians 15:35

But some will say, How are the dead raised up? And with what body do they come?

1 Corinthians 15:39

All flesh *is* not the same flesh: but *there* is *one kind* of flesh of men, another flesh of beasts, another of fishes, *and* another of birds.

1 Corinthians 15:42–44

So also *is* the resurrection of the dead. It is sown in corruption: it is raised in incorruption: It is sown in dishonor; it is raised in glory: it is sown in weakness; it is raised in power: It is sown a natural body; it is raised a spiritual body. There is a natural body. And there is a spiritual body. And so it is written, The first man Adam *was made* a living soul; the last Adam was made a quickening spirit.

1 Corinthians 15:49

And as we have been borne the image of the earthy, we shall also bear image of the heavenly.

Philippians 3:20–21

For our conversation is in heaven; from whence also we look for the Savior, the Lord Jesus Christ: Who shall change our vile body, that it may be fashioned like unto his glorious body, according to the working whereby he is able even to subdue all things unto himself.

Colossians 3:4

When Christ, *who is* our life, shall appear, then shall ye also appear with him in glory.

1 John 3:1-2

Behold, what manner of love the Father hath bestowed upon us, that we should be called the sons of God: therefore the world knoweth us not, because it knew him not. Beloved, now are we the sons of God, and it doth not yet appear what we shall be: but we know that, when he shall appear, we shall be like him; for we shall see him as he is.

Jude 24-25

Now unto him that is able to keep you from falling, and to present *you* faultless before the presence of his glory with exceeding joy. To the only wise God our Saviour, be glory and majesty, dominion and power, both now and ever. Amen.

Revelation 11:15

And the seventh angel sounded; and there were great voices in heaven, saying, The kingdoms of this world are become *the kingdoms* of our Lord, and of his Christ; and he shall reign for ever and ever.

End Notes

[1] My father received his PhD and graduated as the top student in the world, out of a class of forty-four (hand-picked students globally), in the field of Metallurgy at the University of London, England, in 1962. He was then hand-picked by Boeing in Seattle to work on the Apollo Moon missions in 1963. Based on his mathematical genius skills, I asked him to calculate the pre-flood population on earth using a set of parameters. These parameters were based on a world with pristine, pre-flood conditions (healthier nutrients, richer atmosphere, calm weather, less UV rays, etc.). Such a perfect environment included:

- (a) 1,656 years between Adam and Eve to the Great Flood
- (b) An average lifespan of 900 years and half-life of 450 years (as indicated in the lineage of men in Genesis 5)
- (c) A minimum of 15 children per family, ranging to 50 children (each ancient man cited having many "sons and daughters" other than those specifically cited by name)
- (d) It is clearly demonstrated that some post-flood, modern families (having lesser life spans of 75 years) had as many as 14 offspring. Some post-flood, ancient dynasties saw nobility having 50–100 offspring through multiple wives.

Based on my father's mathematical equation, the earth's population would have been a minimum of 200 million to a maximum of 2.5 billion people, with a likely range of 1.5 billion people.

² The process of evolution (evolving) is compatible with God's creation. For instance, the process of a baby evolving through the stages of an embryo and various stages of a fetus is an obvious display of a process of evolution. However, the simple notion of *transitional* evolution, where it is touted that one species can somehow *transition* into another species over immense periods of time (periods of time that are unverifiable) is where the problem lies. This is in direct conflict with God's Word that clearly states that each species brings forth its 'own kind.' And what God has stated in this regard is absolutely verifiable and consistent through the observable evidence.

³ The observable evidence clearly demonstrates that, in the process of procreation, each specific species remains completely intact. No *transitional* life forms have ever been observed within nature, or documented within the observable fossil record. All purported *transitional* life forms, either proclaimed in the recent past or currently proclaimed, have been categorically discounted under rigorous scrutiny (i.e. misleading facts, absence of facts, and, in some cases, complete falsification of facts). All species either adapt to the natural environment or perish due to the natural environment. At the DNA level, adaptations are allowable changes (built in) that help the species to adapt to environmental change. Adaptations do not cause or promote *transitional* change. Mutations, on the other hand, are changes to the DNA that are either 75% harmful or 25% neutral to the sustaining of any particular species. Natural selection preserves the strongest of the species. It *preserves* the species. Natural selection does not allow, or promote, the *transitional* change of any species into some 'other' species that it simply is not.

⁴ The placenta is the link between a pregnant mother and a developing fetus within the womb. It is also a barrier that separates the blood of the fetus from the blood of the host mother. The placenta also acts as a barrier to stop immune system attacks from the host mother. The fetus can be viewed as a 'foreign' life form by the mother's own immune system. Such aggressive attacks can actually trigger a natural, spontaneous abortion. During the 1990s, Immunologist, Dr. Andrew L. Mellor (Medical College of Georgia) determined that an enzyme (IDO) was produced within the placenta to ward off such immune system attacks. On this basis the developing fetus is considered to be a distinct, physical entity separate from its host, maternal mother. The historical bloodline, stemming from Adam (fallen man), is passed on through the union of the male sperm and the female egg. As this physical union did not occur with Mary and

Joseph, Jesus remained in the womb, separate and distinct—and without the fallen nature through sin.

⁵ Although Judas Iscariot was considered to be one of the twelve disciples, he proved in the end that he was never a bonafide disciple. Judas was replaced by Barsabas Matthias as the twelfth disciple (becoming one of the *true* original disciples). This was based on the criteria that the twelfth replacement must have had walked alongside Jesus throughout His ministry and had to be a witness to His crucifixion (Acts 1:21–26).

⁶ American Psychological Association (website); accessed September 2014, www.apa.org/monitor/2014/06/datapoint/aspx. Printed edition News from APA's Center for Workplace Studies, June 2014, Vol. 45, No. 6, p. 13.

"APA's Center for Workforce Studies estimates that as of 2010 there are 93,000 practicing psychologists in the United States. Licensed psychologists totaled approximately 85,000 in 2004. Graduations average 4–5,000 per year and approximately 2,700 of those are in health service provider fields, resulting in an additional 8,100 practicing psychologists." Following this progression there would be over 100,000 practicing psychologists in the U.S. alone by 2015.

⁷ There are basically two main trains of thought regarding the presence of the Holy Spirit after the event of the Rapture. Either the Holy Spirit will remain on earth or the Holy Spirit will be removed. There are compelling arguments on both sides. However, I believe the Holy Spirit will be lifted along with the raptured church, based on the following: (1) The removal of the Holy Spirit allows the Antichrist to be revealed to the remaining world (the presence of the Holy Spirit is currently preventing this from happening); (2) Absolutely devastating and horrifying judgments will occur in earth during the Tribulation period. We are currently witnessing a 'preview' of these calamities as society continues to reject the laws and values of God. This 'spiritual vacuum' allows death and destruction to follow in the absence of the working of the Holy Spirit in the lives of an *increasing* number of people. Basically, the Holy Spirit can be stifled by the rejection of the people. God gave man freedom of choice. And on this basis, (3) there is a distinct reason why God instructs an angel to administer the 'seal of God' in the foreheads of 144,000 chosen and select individuals during the Great Tribulation. I firmly believe that this will be done as a necessary measure because the prevailing protection of the Holy Spirit will be absent at this time.

[8] Currently, the Jewish population is divided into five main segments of religious belief. According the Central Bureau of Statistics of the Jewish population (2010): 8% are Haredi (strictly Orthodox—Old Testament only); 13% are considered Traditional-religious; 25% are considered Traditional; and 42% are considered Secular (non-religious); which leaves 12% in the undecided, or in the 'other' category. Out of this, it is estimated that roughly 350,000 Messianic Jews (2.5% of the population) have proclaimed Yeshua (Hebrew name for Jesus) as Lord and Saviour of their lives. They believe Jesus is the Messiah who has already come. The Orthodox Priests *do not* believe Jesus was the Messiah, and they are still waiting for the Messiah to come. It is interesting that the Orthodox Priests are the modern-day lineage of the Sadducees, Scribes, and Pharisees that mocked and rejected Jesus in the day when He (the Messiah) was standing right in front of the very ones who should have known better. It is also interesting to note that the modern-day Orthodox Priests have plans to resume the burnt/blood offering sacrifices in a future rebuilt temple. They plan this, despite the fact that God, the Father, sent His son Jesus as the *final* sacrifice for all the sins of the world (the Lamb slain from the foundation of the world, Revelation 5:12, 13:8, 21:27). In John 5:43, speaking to the Jewish people, Jesus states that He came in the Father's name, but He would not be received—another will come in his own name (the Antichrist—the false Messiah) and he *will be* received. Also interesting is the fact that it is the Antichrist who persuades the Orthodox Priests to stop the sacrifice and offerings in the future, rebuilt temple (Daniel 9:27). Who else could persuade the Orthodox Priests to stop performing their sacred traditions and rituals? They will most assuredly not listen to anyone but their *perceived* Messiah.

[9] There are many varying opinions regarding the timing of the Rapture. Most believe in a Pre-Tribulation Rapture. Some believe in a Mid-Tribulation Rapture (varying opinions on what 'mid' is actually referring to—the 'middle' of seven years or the 'middle' of three-and-a-half years). Some still adhere to a Post-Tribulation Rapture. And there are a growing number of individuals (notably the proclaimers of Kingdom Now Theology and the New Apostolic Reformation—NAR) who believe there is no such thing as the Rapture. However, after much research and prayer, I have concluded that, first of all, there is going to be a Rapture and, secondly (as spirit-filled believers), we must be praying for the best, but be prepared for the worst-case scenario. I firmly believe the Lord will use His servants on earth right up to the very last minute. The Lord saved both Noah and Lot right at the last minute. So, if that means a Pre-Tribulation

Rapture—so be it. But if it means a Rapture somewhere between Pre and Mid-Tribulation—then we need to be prepared and ready. Remember, by the start of the 'seven-year clock,' anyone can pretty much determine the time of the Second Coming. What we don't know, and not even the angels in heaven know, is the *exact* time (the hour or day) of the Rapture. However, we will know when it is near (in the spirit), "even at the door" (Matthew 24:33–37). When one is 'at the door,' one is moments away from 'opening' the door.

[10] Orthodox and radical followers of the god of Islam, Allah, proclaim that 'infidels' (non-believers of Allah) should be put to death by way of beheading. The Bible indicates that, in the end times, those who are martyred by proclaiming the name of Jesus will be beheaded (Revelation 20:4). In fact, beheadings of Christians in the Middle East and Northern Africa are occurring right now in the name of Allah and Islam. Another interesting fact is that the name of Allah can be traced back to ancient civilizations who worshipped the 'Moon god.' Is it coincidental that one of the main symbols of Islam is the crescent moon? Allah and Jehovah are not the same (Allah does not have a Son). Jesus is only referred to as a 'prophet' in the Qur'an. Remember, at the Rapture, only born-again Christians are removed—unbelievers (and the undecided) are left behind. It is out of the *undecided* that there will be those who will make a clear decision and are beheaded for the witness of Jesus Christ. God does not discriminate against heritage, or nationality. He wishes that none should perish, but instead receive everlasting life through salvation in Jesus Christ (John 3:16; Acts 4:10–12; 1 John 4.3).

[11] Quoted from the "First Book of Enoch" 22:9–12, Ethiopic Text, Richard Lawrence, published 1821.

[12] The First Book of Enoch clearly presents the Messiah, the Saviour who takes away the sins of the world and who will cast judgment and establish His kingdom upon the Earth at the end of this age. This is described in 1 Enoch 46:1–4, 48, 48A, and 50. Jesus is referred to as the "Son of man" (capital S), the "Elect One," and the "Concealed One" in the context of having been with the "Ancient of days" and the "Lord of spirits" (God, the Father) since the very beginning, before the earth was created. Not only was Enoch the first person to be raptured, he was the first to see Jesus, the Son of man, prior to His First Coming.

¹³ It needs to be stated that there are different circumstances and parameters regarding the mention of trumpets in Scripture. In most cases, especially in ancient times, the sounding of a trumpet is the signal of a specific announcement. There are three variations of trumpets: (1) human, (2) angelic, and (3) Divine. There is a distinct difference between the 'trumpets' sounded by angels and the 'trump of God' (Divine). In Revelation (21) judgments occur during the Tribulation period. There are seven seals, seven trumpets, and seven bowls. The first four of the seven seals mark the first half of the seven-year Tribulation. If you look closely at the seven trumpets (that follow the last of the seals), they are sounded by angels, and looking even closer they seem to announce the forthcoming seven bowls. These interlocking trumpets and bowls occur during the very traumatic and intense latter half of the seven-year period—known as the Great Tribulation. The last of the seven trumpets, sounded by an angel, marks the announcement of the Second Coming of Christ to earth (Zephaniah 1:14–16, Joel 2:1, Revelation 11:15). This is confirmed in Matthew 24:29–31 where Jesus sends forth His angels to separate the left-behind remnant under first heaven—announced by a trumpet (the last of the seven) and to claim the kingdoms of the earth. The unrighteous will fully see Him returning and will mourn at His coming. Conversely, at the 'trump of God' where the righteous are raptured, it is only these specific individuals that will see Him and they will fully rejoice when they do. The divine 'trump of God' is only mentioned at two specific events within Scripture: (1) the calling of Moses to the mountain to meet with God (Exodus 19:16–25) and (2) at the Rapture where the righteous saved meet the Son of God (1 Thessalonians 4:16). The latter being the announcement of the redeemed and raptured church 'bride' and the beginning of the Tribulation period that ushers in the (21) judgments—including the seven trumpets sounded by angels.

¹⁴ There is a train of thought that the term 'paradise' spoken of in Luke 23:43 is referring to the "side of rest" in Hades (Abraham's Bosom) where the pre-Cross deceased (those not in hell) and the future post-Rapture deceased (those not in hell) await their resurrection (the First Resurrection). There is the other train of thought that the term 'paradise' is referring to the Kingdom of Heaven (third heaven). This is based on Revelation 2:7 that states that the "Tree of Life" (once located in the midst of the Garden of Eden) is now located in the "midst of the paradise of God" (the Kingdom of Heaven). I firmly believe the latter viewpoint, also confirmed and based on the distinct description of the Kingdom of Heaven in Revelation 22:1–2 and 22:14–15. In addition, there

are divergent views that Jesus meant that the crucified criminal would see 'paradise' *today* (that very day)—or that Jesus told him *today* he would see 'paradise' (indicating a possible future day). However, considering the point made in this book, the timeline really doesn't matter, because the newly born-again criminal (upon death on his own cross) became asleep in Jesus (on that very day). On this basis, being in the body of Christ, the deceased criminal would in fact be with Jesus when He descended to Hades (for those 3 days) and then would in fact be in 'paradise' (the Kingdom of Heaven) upon ascension—to be subsequently awakened at the event of the coming Rapture. Bear in mind that Jesus did not refer to 'paradise' in any way in "the parable of the rich man and Lazarus" in Luke chapter 16. He definitely spoke of Abraham's Bosom (the side of rest in Hades), *not* the Kingdom of Heaven.

[15] There is another train of thought that proclaims the 'sons of God' (Genesis 6) are not 'fallen angels,' but are instead mortal men from the lineage of Seth. There are serious problems with this doctrine of belief. If this were true, then: (1) how did the genetic corruption occur that produced Nephilim giants "in those days" (the days *prior* to flood)? (2) How did the genetic corruption occur that produced Nephilim giants "also after that" (the days *after* the flood)? (3) Why would God's Word differentiate between the '*sons* of God' and the 'daughters of *men*'? Why not the 'sons of *men*' choosing the 'daughters of *men*'? (4) Why would God save Noah, his sons and all their wives (and other select, uncontaminated life forms) from the destruction of the world (to eradicate all the remaining genetic contamination of all types of flesh) and then allow this genetic corruption to begin to repeat itself (post-flood) *directly* as a result from their own *supposed* corrupt, genetic state—since they were of the lineage of Seth (stemming from Adam)? Consider that Noah was "*perfect* in his generations" (emphasis added). The word 'perfect' is derived from the Hebrew word *Tamiym*, meaning, 'without blemish' or 'undefiled' which is referring to being 'genetically perfect' (not physically corrupt). The 'corrupted flesh' cited in Genesis 6 is referring to a physical, genetic corruption—not *specifically* referring to the fallen spiritual nature, or a state of sin. And despite this fact, we must still recognize that it was the fallen nature of sinful man that was a foundational premise that led up to an eventual state of genetic corruption in the first place. Although Noah "walked with God" and was "a just man," Noah and the others were not 'sinless.' They were still in need of redemption and salvation. (5) The 'sons of God' presented themselves before the Lord and *Satan* (the now-fallen angel Lucifer, *not* Lucifer before the fall)

was among them (Job 1:6). How is it possible that mortal men (the sons of Seth) were able to present themselves before the throne room of God in third heaven? (6) In Job 38:4–7 God replies to Job, saying, "Where was he when He laid the foundations of earth" (man was not yet created, and therefore, could not have witnessed the creation of the earth). However, the morning stars (God's loyal angels) sang together, and the 'sons of God' (the *identified*, and soon to be, disloyal angels prior to the fall) shouted for joy when *they* all collectively witnessed the creation of the earth. How could the 'sons of Seth' (mortal men) witness the creation unfolding, if they are in fact the direct descendants of Adam?

[16] Quoted from the First Book of Enoch 15:8–9, Ethiopic Text, Richard Lawrence, published 1821.

[17] Pertaining to the death of an individual, 'clinically dead' refers to the cessation of breathing and blood circulation known as cardiac arrest. In this stage, full restoration of the brain can occur within three minutes. Beyond three minutes, increased risk of resulting brain damage will occur. Other organs of the body can survive without damage up to six hours. The term 'medically dead' or 'brain dead' refers to a total cessation of brain activity leading to an eventual total and permanent cessation of all other body functions (barring any artificial organ assistance).

[18] The book "The Boy Who Came Back from Heaven" (2010) described the story of Alex Malarkey who, at age six, recounts his visit to heaven after he suffered a car accident in 2004. In January 2015, Alex Malarkey retracted his story, claiming, "*I did not die. I did not go to heaven. I said I went to heaven because I thought it would get me attention. When I made the claims that I did, I had never read the Bible. People have profited from lies, and continue to. They should read the Bible, which is enough. The Bible is the only source of truth. Anything written by man cannot be infallible.*" **The book has been subsequently pulled from publication and various bookstore shelves.**

[19] Before Christ's death on the Cross, an annual cleansing of sin occurred on the tenth day of the seventh month known as Yom Kippur—the Day of Atonement. It was recognized that only God could alleviate the great burden of the weight of guilt, shame, and regret from the accumulation of sin committed by the people. Since it was God who created all things and through His creation

provided all things needed to sustain life, a selected animal—a sacrifice—was given back to God as a way of thanks and to reconcile the sins of the people. The selected animal had to be unblemished (genetically perfect). It had to be the best of the flock. Unsurprisingly, Satan perverted the sacrifice. Through the worship of false gods (fallen angels) Satan caused ancient man to increase the sacrifice from yearly to daily. He caused ancient man to increase the number of offerings. He caused ancient man to offer up human sacrifice beyond animal sacrifice offerings. We see this clearly in ancient cultures, such as the Mayans, where human sacrifice was a daily occurrence. The Mayans worshiped Q'uq'umatz, the 'feathered snake god.' The Aztecs worshipped Quetzalcoatl, the 'feathered serpent god.' And the Incas worshipped Viracocha, the 'feathered serpent god.' Remember, Satan was the winged angel Lucifer and had transformed into a *serpent* at the Garden of Eden. This perversion and false worship, leading to increased sin and genetic contamination, is what caused God to destroy the world by a global flood in Noah's time. So God sent Jesus Christ as the last, final, and complete sacrifice for the sins of mankind. This is why Jesus is referred to as the "Lamb of God" (with a capital L). Today, we give 'thanks' for our meals by offering a prayer of thanks for the sacrifice of the various living things provided by God through His creation—living things we consume in order to sustain ourselves. So, God is not only the creator of all things, He is the provider of all things—including salvation.

[20] One example has been demonstrated in this book (pages 29–30) that the translation of the word 'world' in Matthew 24:3 should read 'an age' derived from the Greek word *Aion*. Obviously, after Armageddon, through the Thousand Year Reign of Christ the 'world' does not end. God recreates the Heavens and Earth after the Great White Throne Judgment—so it is a 'world' without end. Another example of the incidental errors of translation is the statement in Exodus 20:13, "Thou shalt not kill." The word 'kill' is derived from the Hebrew word *ratsach*, meaning the act of murder. This commandment should read, "Thou shalt not [commit] murder." This is in the context of taking a life without just cause (conversely, any person has the right to defend themselves). However, the early translators may have been greatly influenced by the centuries of brutal warfare and gruesome inquisitions prior to the advent of the King James Bible.

Bibliography

Recommended Books

Preparing for Eternity: Do We Trust God's Word or Religious Traditions? Mike Gendron, Northhampton Press, 2011

The Evidence for Creation: Examining the Origin of Planet Earth Dr. G.S. McLean – Roger Oakland – Larry McLean, Full Gospel Bible Institute, 1989

The Signature of God: Astonishing Biblical Discoveries Grant R. Jeffrey, Frontier Research, 1996

Signature in the Cell: DNA and the Evidence for Intelligent Design Dr. Stephen Meyer, Harper One, 2009

America B.C.: Ancient Settlers in the New World Barry Fell, Quadrangle/New York Times Book Co., 1976

What in the World is Going On? 10 Prophetic Clues You Can't Afford to Ignore Dr. David Jeremiah, Thomas Nelson, 2008

Pagan Christianity: Exploring the Roots of Our Church Practices
Frank Viola – George Barna, BarnaBooks, 2008

Recommended Websites

Understand the Times, International – Roger Oakland
www.understandthetimes.org

The Berean Call – Tom McMahon – Dave Hunt (deceased)
www.thebereancall.org

Proclaiming the Gospel – Mike Gendron
www.pro-gospel.org

Got Questions? Bible Questions Answered
www.gotquestions.org

Creation Evidence Museum of Texas – Dr. Carl Baugh
www.creationevidence.org

Canopy Ministries – James Gardner
www.canopyministries.org

Recommended DVD Series

In Search of the Truth of Origins
Roger Oakland – order online at www.understandthetimes.org

About the Author

After pursuing a career in music in the United States, Mark returned to Canada, eventually settling in Saskatchewan. Rebuilding his life, Mark experienced various lines of work, from major construction to becoming a financial advisor in the Credit Union system to being a senior sales consultant in retail to working with a national courier service. All through this time, Mark began to receive revelations from God—starting in 1986, with a major revelation received in May of 1988.

Since those early years, Mark recognized that he was a sinner. He has declared and has received Jesus Christ as Lord and Savior of his life. He married and started a family and continued to pursue research and study of God's Word in the areas of Eschatology and Creation research during the early 1990s. For over twenty-seven years, some twelve thousand hours of research and study have been logged in.

After attending various conferences, Mark was inspired to develop multiple presentations (based on both his own research and the collective research of others). Mark has presented these at speaking seminars to the general public over a period of four years. Plans are currently being made to develop these presentations into DVD format in the near future.

Mark was led by the Holy Spirit to write this book as a first step. Along with the future development of the presentations in DVD format, a second book is currently in the early development stage.

All of this will be collectively presented and offered through a ministry website under Search Light Presentation Ministry. The desired goal is to share the validity of the Word of God, demonstrating the Spiritual nature of man and the validity of the coming event of the Rapture fulfilling the redeemed church under Christ for all eternity.

Search Light Presentation Ministry

Launching Website in the Spring of 2016
www.slpmsk.org

Website Features:
- Declaring the almighty, sovereign God as revealed in the Scriptures of the Bible
- Declaring Jesus Christ as Lord of lords, and King of kings
- Declaring the Holy Spirit that teaches and leads us into all truth and righteousness
- Revealing the validity and purpose of Prophecy
- Revealing the truth of Creation through His Word, confirmed through quantified scientific principles and unchanging universal laws
- Revealing a deeper understanding of the Word over all and to ignite excitement, a hunger and thirst, for the deeper things of the Spirit
- Presenting and promoting various researchers of the Word and providing a central website with external links to encourage ongoing personal research and discovery of Spiritual revelations

A consistent thread that weaves throughout these seven features is a call to warn of the spiritual deception that is occurring in these last days. Some areas of deception are plain to see, while others are not as easily discerned. It is the intention of this website to help open the eyes of the spiritually blind.

Mark G. Toop
Founder

CPSIA information can be obtained
at www.ICGtesting.com
Printed in the USA
LVOW04s0202031216
515581LV00012B/159/P

9 781486 610655